Signals on Fire

A HEARTBRIDGE

ISBN-13: 978-1721223473
ISBN-10: 1721223479

BISAC:
Biography & Autobiography / People with Disabilities

Editing by Gina Paris and Alexandria Page

Design and illustrations by Artline Graphics, Sedona AZ, USA
www.artline-graphics.com

Signals on Fire

A HEARTBRIDGE

Lavina Jeane Page

In loving memory of

Brady Sloan Paris

Dedicated to Brady's parents,
Gina and Billy,
and his siblings, Charlie and Riley.
And to all those who knew and loved Brady.

Acknowledgments

This book has developed out of a series of life experiences that seem to have been fated to take place within my family. It is for this reason that I would like to give special thanks to these individuals who made this book and remembrance possible.

I would like to acknowledge Billy and Gina for their continued and steadfast support throughout the eight months that it took me to write this book. They unremittingly put out all my fires along the way, and it was only with their expertise and patience that I was able to navigate the computer and refine the skills needed to write and organize my thoughts into a book. Not only did Gina lend her support throughout the process of writing this memoir, but she was an integral part of the editing process. I am forever grateful for the time she spent assisting me with recalling details and organizing and editing this work.

The bond of siblings is immeasurable, and without Charlie and Riley some of these stories about their brother would not be possible. The pride and energy I've experienced from being their grandmother is unparalleled, and I cannot imagine this journey without the vivacity that surrounds them.

Admittedly, the amount of operator-created errors during this process was no small number. For this reason, I would also like to thank my sons, Bobby and Adam. It was their unrelenting willingness to troubleshoot any and all unforeseen technical issues I encountered that enabled me to carry on my work with minimal disruption. They were even dedicated enough as my personal information technology team to remote log-in and perform repairs on several occasions.

I would also like to recognize my daughter, Alexandria. Her passion and creativity allowed me to see the beauty in writing and empowered me to properly convey my gratitude to everyone who has made an impact on the transformation of this vision. Ultimately, without her having given up so much of her time and expertise to edit and fine-tune this book I would have never crossed the finish line.

A special thanks to Elizabeth Martina Bishop for giving me the support and push I needed to write this book, coaching me through this process, and helping with the editing process. Furthermore, I wish to express my gratitude for Anugito ten Voorde of Artline Graphics for designing the perfect cover, formatting my manuscript, and producing a beautiful representation of my memories.

Finally, I would to thank my mother for teaching me that I could do anything and be anything I wanted; it was her example of strength and wisdom that brought me to this point in my life.

Light of Day

To those who helped me on the way,
To surrender all to their play.
They came in force to help their way,
To bring this book to the stage.
With grateful thanks to those who came,
To help this book see the light of day.

Table of Contents

PART I

Introduction

Secret Journal

Secret Journal

It was an otherwise dreary day. As she was going through her bookshelf and searching for something to read, she knew she wanted a book that would be inspiring and lift her spirits. She loved to read and enjoyed looking through many different types of books. Even more so, she liked touching the various textures of their covers one at a time; the experience reminded her of how she felt when she saw bolts of material in a fabric shop. They were all so different in color, style, and texture. It was the feel of the fabrics that brought her pleasure. Her books were no different and brought her the same great delight.

Her collection referenced many different topics, as her interests ranged from action and adventure stories to other books of a more spiritual nature. She touched each one and admired its cover and name as she sifted through them. One book in particular seemed to jump out and beg for her attention, it was drawing her in. In fact, the book called her by name. It was more of a soft, gentle whisper that she heard; she could have sworn the words were, *Gum Gum.*

No, that can't be, can it? Her interest was piqued now, "this must be the book I need to read today," she said to herself.

As she reached for it she saw that it was a different book, a new book; one that she had never seen before. The leather hardcover was a deep burgundy color and a

11

golden infinity symbol was embossed on the spine. Its gilded pages shimmered in the morning light.

At first, she thought the book was an ancient text, but as she drew closer she could see that it wasn't. Instead, the book had more of an ageless appearance to it. With curiosity and great care, she pulled the book from the shelf. As she held it in her hands she noticed the shape of a dolphin and the image of a golden pen were stamped on the front cover.

The golden dolphin was swimming in electric blue iridescent water that had the liquid smooth movement of mercury, as light shone down through the clouds and caressed the dolphin. The streaming sunlight gave her the impression of something almost otherworldly, which she liked.

As she began tracing the beautiful golden dolphin with her finger, she was reminded of her grandson. She had a grandson named Brady who had enjoyed swimming with dolphins and had done so on two occasions. He had been gone for over five years and the loss tugged at her heart whenever she thought of him.

As she followed the outline of the dolphin with her index finger, the book seemed to come alive. It began glowing with a radiant light. As the colors of the water and the dolphin grew bolder and brighter, there were hints of movement that continued in both. Meanwhile, she noticed the golden pen hung suspended in midair just above the dolphin. It was as if the pen was alive and anxiously waiting for someone to pick it up and begin writing.

As she held the book in her trembling hands, she felt

transfixed by the scene unfolding before her eyes. In disbelief, she blinked and decided she must be imagining things that were not really happening. When she opened her eyes, the book in all of its radiance was still glowing in her hands. She felt as if she were being pulled into the energy of the book. There was a force behind the energy that practically demanded she pay close attention to what was transpiring, yet she felt a gentle firmness that encouraged her to begin reading this book and no other.

She didn't know where this book came from, she only knew that it had not been purchased by her. It was as if it had appeared out of nowhere and landed on her bookshelf. As she examined it more closely, she began to realize it was more of a journal than a book. *A beautiful journal of someone who must have been very special,* she thought. She could feel the love radiating from the journal. Now, the love spread to her hands, arms, and body as she held the glowing book. This was a gentle love that warmed and lifted her spirits.

She very gingerly opened the journal, curious to know more. She also wanted to savor all the feelings and sensations she was experiencing. As she opened it, a burst of light particles surged out and surrounded her.

It was as if the energy that had long been held inside the book had finally been released. She felt as though the journal had been waiting just for her to discover. *How long had it been waiting for her?* She didn't know and didn't care. She was only certain that this must have been the exact moment for her to come across the journal.

Upon opening the journal, she noticed one word materializing through the radiant light: **BRADY.** Chills coursed up her spine and her body trembled as she gazed at the one word. Tears flooded her eyes and a sudden *knowing* filled her heart. *How could this be?*

It was all starting to make sense to her now. The dolphin and golden pen on the cover...Brady may have even written the journal with the golden pen. She excitedly flipped through the pages of the journal just to be sure it was Brady's, already knowing as she did that it was. He had even called her by name—Gum Gum. The pieces were starting to come together.

She saw that entries had been made in the journal, and they were from a perspective that no one else would be privy to. They were recollections that noted places Brady had visited, the things he had done, the people in his life, and dealing with members of his family. Most importantly, he wanted to share his life and his love with his family, with everyone.

It was an enigma to her how his dolphin journal found its way to her bookshelf, but she didn't try to understand it. In her mind, this was the stuff of mysteries, fairytales, and illusion. All she knew was that Brady had found a way to put it on her bookshelf; she was destined to find it. It would be Brady's secret as to how he wrote his story and included it in her collection.

PART II

Brady

My name is Brady

My Dolphin Journal

Brady's Message

My Name is Brady

This is the beginning of a special book—my journal. It details many stories that happened in my life as a not so ordinary boy. The entire book is about me, Brady. Right now, I'm sitting here under an apple tree that is ripe with delicious looking ruby red apples. I'm getting ready to write the details of my untold story in a journal that was given to me as a gift when I first arrived in this place.

Where exactly am I now? I have come to a place not so far from home, somewhere between worlds; some may call it heaven. I can feel a light whispering in the wind. It's filled with many pastel shades—pink, blue, and white hues whirl amidst the ether, creating a heavenly, peaceful paradise around me.

I feel wonderful over here on the other side of life. My body is lighter than air and I have no aches or pains. I know I can do everything a guy could ever want to do. I can run quick like a rabbit, eat, and savor the delicious ruby red apples; I can talk, SHOUT, or even whisper. I am able to listen and hear every sound in the universe. I can hear birds chirping, my grandma's voice, you name it—I can hear it. I can also see the most beautiful things with such clarity that I was never able to perceive during my short stay on Earth.

★★★

Over here, I have many friends. Some of my friends are angels; they are pretty cool. The angels know I have had an affinity for dolphins ever since a wild dolphin swam up to me, kissed my toes, and tickled my feet (this happened while I was swimming in the ocean when I was eight years old). Knowing my love for dolphins, my friends gave me a special book—a journal—featuring one on the cover, and a golden pen. I was told that with these gifts I needed to write my story in the dolphin journal with the golden pen. I was to include anything that I might remember of my transition into my new life here in heaven. Any event I witnessed or felt after I came here was to be incorporated. Before I wrote with gold lettering in my journal, I was told that it would act as a tribute to those I left behind and validate the life I experienced.

Now, it appears as though my friends have given me a monumental homework assignment: journal your earthly experiences! The strange thing is, all the suffering and excitement that I once experienced in the physical form are now starting to fade from my mind. My life now feels like it all happened to someone else, or as if my life was all part of a dream. I don't want these memories of mine to fade into nothingness so I'm going to complete this assignment!

★★★

How do I begin writing about myself? I want to let you know, I've never composed any kind of journal before because I wasn't capable of writing while I lived on Earth; I couldn't even move a muscle in a purposeful way. I'm not sure if I even know how to write in the here and now.

I know that I'm present in this celestial realm and I'm occupying a new ethereal form, but I'm not used to being here yet. This place is so different from my other home. It should be interesting to see how this new writing develops and if I get the hang of it quickly. I have a chance to do some journaling now so I'm going to try using my new pen and see what happens.

I opened up my journal while wondering to myself, "how am I ever to accomplish this huge undertaking?" My recollections are disappearing fast. I picked up my golden pen and there was suddenly a flash of light with pictures of my former life appearing in front of me, as if they were part of a movie sequence. I noticed a shift taking place inside me. "This is no ordinary pen," I thought; "this is a MAGICAL PEN!"

I was momentarily stunned by the flashing picture show appearing in my mind. At this point, I dropped the pen. Soon after releasing it I realized that I didn't have to worry about my thoughts evaporating into thin air, as long as I hold the magical golden pen in my hand. I think I now understand a little better how it works; the imprint of my own special signature is embedded in the golden pen. Each time I pick it up, pictures and movies of my past life on Earth, and this new heavenly life, are activated in my mind's eye.

With this elegant golden pen in my hand I enjoyed watching the many memories quickly flashing through my mind. In fact, these scenes seemed so vivid and real, I wanted to hold onto them forever; I wanted these memory movies woven into the essence of my being so that in time I won't need the golden pen to remember them.

The images are playing in my mind at this very moment. I have a new understanding that I can easily draw upon these beautiful movies whenever I want to visit my family and remember my time on Earth.

As I watched the brilliant pictures flicker before me, I saw that I was only fifteen years old. How I knew this, I don't know; I just did. I also knew that I was supposed to journal the details of the movies that were displayed by my magical pen. The memories that I was shown to write down were dependent on my mood and reflected the same feeling in that particular moment of my earthly experience. These cherished recollections reminded me that in my former life I would evoke memories to cheer myself up. Upon realizing this, I can't help but smile. Since my body mirrored how I felt in a reflection, I experienced the sensations of the earthly me all over again, but from my new vantage point.

The minute I picked up the golden pen, I felt love flowing through me. I was overcome by joy and an intense gratitude for the gift of having known my amazing earthly family. I treasured all these crazy, wonderful people that had been part of my life. I wanted to find a way in which to share these remarkable events with my parents, grandparents, siblings, and the many other people I had known.

As the first scene played in my mind, I saw the uniqueness of each person. This uniqueness was similar to a key. The roles these people played in my life served as the key that unlocked their very special gifts. These gifts would be shared with me or another person whenever it was needed. By the giving and sharing of the keys to each other's gifts, and doing so with love, we were bound together as a very close-knit family. That was how we were able to get through the difficult and challenging years. We made it look easy to the outside world, didn't we?

All my memories came flooding back to me. The longer I hold the golden pen, the more things I can remember. I enjoy thinking about my love for my family; I lived for and thrived on those thoughts. I have a better understanding why I had decided to stay on Earth after I was born–love. Love was the glue that held my family together. Love is the glue that holds the entire world together as one family.

I suddenly realized that I still have the same gift that I did on Earth, of being able to view other people's memories of me with great insight. I know what thoughts people need to help them develop their hidden talents. I had the ability to see beyond the physical and into the intricate workings of each particular soul. I know what each individual in my family needs most and I would go over each and every memory–old and new. Those memories helped me in the most trying of times, as they reminded me of why I was ever present in a physical form and of the love I had for the job I was there to do. I wanted everyone to remember the happy times, not just the miserable and trying times, so I can and would tweak the memories a little in my favor.

I thought to myself, "how funny, it seems like yesterday and yet it feels like there is no time when it comes to memories. Memories are in the now time, real time happening all over again."

I want you to know that we all have the chance to re-live the joys of our lives through meaningful snapshot pictures occurring in our minds. Through those pictures, once again, feel the love of our families and friends and send our love and healing thoughts to them through our remembrances. Tweak the memories a little if you have to, keep them sweet! These memories, filled with love, are the healing balm underlying all things. Regardless of what you may think is of importance, these are also someone else's memories and you want them to be beautiful from their perspective too.

I know how the golden pen works now, as it provides me with a great moving picture show of my past. Let's see if I know how to put words on paper. I pick it up and set it to the first page in my journal. As soon as I set pen to the paper, a miraculous thing happened. The picture movie began, and the golden pen started moving on the paper–I am actually writing in my dolphin journal! I did-n't have to learn how to write, I already knew how.

My Dolphin Journal

Entry 1: 1997

Stand in Faith or Crumble in Fear

My parents and grandparents were all very anxious and scared for me. Everyone came together and rooted for me from the minute I was born. They operated as one unified forcefield. When I was born there was a problem, so the doctors were quick to call a family meeting. The doctors then made a startling announcement that all had to do with me. The doctors were talking about me, Brady. The words flew over my head as if sparrows were carrying messages from above. The doctors said to my family, "you are naïve and in shock, you cannot fully understand what the term *critical care* really means."

Yes, of course, the doctors knew what kind of a state I was in. In fact, I could go back home at any moment and it would not be a decision on my part, nor on anybody else's. It just was how things stood since the day I was born. The whole body could shut down. I just couldn't imagine leaving my beautiful family members, I felt as if I would betray my family by giving up and leaving them. It wasn't my decision, though; someone else held the keys to my future.

Doctors don't always know everything. At this point, it seemed clear to me that my parents and grandparents knew a higher power was at work here. That divinity would be our source of strength; not just for me, but for everyone else too. Because of that *knowing* of a higher power, each family member trusted that they would move forward with me and help me stay alive.

I would play a distinct role in their lives; I would belong to them. That sense of belonging could not be cut off just like that. Every family member, including me, carried a piece—a sacred key—to a mysterious puzzle. We were all bound together by spirit and held a secure and united front against what was to come in the years that were to follow. That was for sure.

My parents never let the doctors get to them. They didn't give the doctors at the hospital a second thought. Actually, it's probably good that my family could only see what they felt was truly possible and didn't entertain any negative thoughts or 'what ifs.' Otherwise, it might have crushed my family beyond repair or left them scarred for life.

★★★

Maybe my parents and grandparents only knew how to stay in just that one moment; that one moment that everyone has at least once in their lifetime. *The one moment of… is it life or death? Is it love or be loved? Is it stay or fold? Is it stand in your faith or crumble in fear? Is it trust or be trusted? Is it hate or forgive? Is it cry tears of joy for yourself or tears for others?* In that moment, I believe my parents and grandparents chose and went beyond the simple words. I believe they went to the source of all things–the God within each one of us. Whether that was a conscious or unconscious decision, it doesn't really matter. They didn't take from doctors or from others' beliefs. My parents and grandparents chose from the love within their hearts, from what was possible in their minds and hearts and held to it, and so did I.

Spark
I am so little. How can that be,
That joyous spark lives inside of me.

Entry 2: 1997

Warrior Spirit

The doctors told my family about my physical condition and what was required to care for me; it was a tricky thing for them to juggle all my special needs. You see, I was special in every way. My grandmother had always known I was going to be special. She had a premonition, but she didn't even know the half of it. I just wanted to give her a heads up, so she could be prepared to help me in the way I needed to be helped. I also wanted her to be prepared for just how much help I was going to need. To be fair though, I really didn't tell her everything; I knew her purpose and I edited out the most difficult parts of my life.

I saw my grandma as a special person, a person who was here on Earth to offer my parents the very comfort they needed. My parents birthed me, they would feel things in a very deep way and would need inspiration and encouragement.

You see, I almost didn't stay with my family members even though I wanted to. I felt the pull to go back home. At times, I felt it was much too hard to stay. Meanwhile, my magnificent warrior spirit rose up inside me; it was that same warrior spirit that was always there with me and with my family. I had a lot to teach my parents and grandparents, as well as the siblings that came along later. I didn't want to miss out on any of it. I knew I had a job to do–this was my assignment. I would be lying if I told you I never felt like giving up. I couldn't tell anyone how I really felt.

Entry 3: 1997

Gum Gum and Me

My grandmother, usually referred to as Gum Gum, lived a block away from me. She came to my house and took care of me on a regular basis; I was very glad for this. Every time she came to take care of me, I felt blessed.

★★★

Gum Gum truly loved me. She used to rock and rock me. While she was rocking me, she gave over her heart to praying; praying for me to stay. I know she feared that I might suddenly leave whenever she was alone with me. I knew if that ever happened, it would break her heart. That is why I clung to her. She used all her strength and love to help keep me very much alive and in my body.

★★★

Gum Gum used to tell me not to do anything silly. "Don't even think of leaving us," she used to say. Later, she would rock and hold me close to her. When she held me close to her, my whole being filled up with the warmth of her arms and the healing nature of her love, which seemed to permeate the entire room. During those times of great silence, I used to sense a strange light coming out of nowhere. The light would enter down deep into my very soul. I felt everything about her presence was very important–the love, the tears, and the awesomeness of the great healing power that she held within her being.

Entry 4: 1998

Overcoming Awkwardness

Before my grandmother came to know me, she always felt uncomfortable around children and adults with disabilities. It certainly wasn't because she didn't care for them. What was really going on was that she didn't know what to say to them, or what to say to their caregivers either. She also told me she was very afraid of saying the wrong thing and having her words appear disrespectful or hurtful in any way.

My grandma didn't like feeling this particular way and always wanted to edit out her thoughts. She knew that this wasn't the right way to carry on thinking, but just didn't know how to overcome this awkwardness she felt. I think the years of taking care of me, and going to a children's hospital with me, helped her; she saw many special needs children–especially at the children's hospital. There were many kids there who were in a much worse state than I was. I find that difficult to imagine, but it's perfectly true.

★★★

Slowly, throughout many years of being exposed to special needs children, and especially because of her contact with me, my grandma began to change. In those places where she used to feel awkward, uncomfortable, shy, or tongue-tied, she was now able to interact with ease and compassion—everything felt perfectly natural to her. It didn't matter whether it was a child or an adult; whatever the challenge was, Gum Gum could meet it head-on.

Entry 5: 2000

The Deliciousness of Gum

My grandmother was also known as Gum Gum, but for me, she was always just Grandma. Shortly after my sister Charlie was born, Grandma went and acquired the name Gum Gum. Around the time Charlie started talking, my grandmother would sometimes offer her gum. This became a regular thing for her to do, even though my mother wasn't so keen on this offering. Eventually my little brother Riley came along, and Grandma continued with that tradition. Each time my brother and sister would catch sight of my grandma, they would cry out in unison, "GUM GUM!" I used to hear them calling out to her, waiting for her magic gift of gum. You know how kids are.

To be fair though, neither my brother nor my sister

could pronounce the word "grandma." So, Gum Gum was Grandma's new name. That was a name that stuck like gum on a shoe. The name Gum Gum moved through the family to the point that it wasn't long before others were calling Grandma the same thing. On the other hand, I knew her before this nickname was ever given to her, so Grandma was really how I thought of her. On occasion, though, I would slip up and, in my head, hear myself say, "Gum Gum!" In those moments I would have to laugh at myself. Why was that? I had never chewed gum or known the deliciousness of it, otherwise I may have been inclined to call her that too.

★★★

Gum Gum knew all about how to take very good care of me, how to feed me, and how to give me my medicines; she knew what I needed and when I needed it. She also knew the way I should be positioned in bed or in my wheelchair. She knew how to suction me, how to get me to cough up a serious plug of mucus that could knock me out. She knew how to dress me. Basically, she knew how to take care of my every need.

Once in a while it would get scary for her, especially if I was choking up real bad and she was alone with me. She kept her cool though, and if she lost it and needed help she would yell one word only. "GINA!" In a tone that Mom knew meant, "come now!" Soon enough they would have me back on track again.

Entry 6: 2001

The Secret Room

In the beginning, when I was first born, we lived in a different house than we do now. It was an old two-story house near a lake, not the one we live in now. It was rather noisy with me and my valets living in an open space that was meant for the entire family. We moved so there would be more room and privacy for me and my valets.

In the big new house that was set back in the woods I had my own private suite. My mother went and remodeled the bathroom so that my shower chair could be rolled into the shower without too much effort. There was a kitchenette installed where my vitamins, formula cans, and all my medicines could be stored and prepared. The valets had a small room with a TV in it where they could fill out their nursing reports without disturbing me while I was resting in my room.

There was another little space off my bedroom that my mom used as a sewing room. One day, long after my aunt and uncle moved out of Gum Gum's house, Mom gave that room to my grandma to sleep in. Gum Gum's door was the door located right next to mine. I know she liked being next to me, she could hear everything that went on in my room. Sometimes at night if I was coughing or having trouble, she would come in and help the valet and stay until she knew I was feeling better. It felt good knowing that my Gum Gum was right there beside me, at my beck and call. I felt she was magical–like a fairy grandmother.

Entry 7: 1997

The Ugly Truth

Even though my grandmother knew what I was going to be like before I was born, she never told anyone. How could she tell her daughter or anyone else? Even though the truth of my life made her feel as though she had been kicked in the stomach (when I communicated with her), I told her how things would really be. I told her the truth, and the truth was ugly.

Grandma knew there was nothing she could do to change the outcome of my birth. That didn't mean she ever gave up; she always tried to do something to change how things were. Prior to my birth, she knew exactly what would happen and carried this grave sorrow. I know she wondered why she was privy to this *knowing* if she couldn't change the outcome. It is only now that everything makes sense to her. The reason wasn't so she could change anything; the purpose was so that I would have someone I could connect with in this life. Someone that could feel me, hear me, see me, and know I was with her even when she could not physically be with me.

When I needed to, I could go to my grandmother for

spiritual comfort. Or if she needed guidance, I could also help her on the spiritual levels I knew how to navigate so well.

Entry 8: 1997

Beauty's Maternal Face

My mother's beauty was in her love for me. She showed her love in the way she cradled me in her arms with a kind of love that passed all boundaries of heart and soul. The delicate and sensitive way in which she cared for me was demonstrated with a soft, feathery-light touch. I felt like her little baby chick for sure.

I know she wondered how she would take care of this sweet boy; this special little boy that was in her life now. I'll tell you how she did it–with an ease and grace that only she could show. She kept everything running smoothly and made it look easy when it was not. Her common-sense way of handling any crisis was her gift and her strength.

Her level of perseverance and dedication was amazing in and of itself; she met every challenge in our lives head-on. She and I knew that it had been our plan all along to be in each other's lives. We were a perfect fit for each other from the very beginning.

The Love We Share
As roses bloom in the light,
Your love showed through in spite of the night.
Your hugs and kisses you freely gave.
You cradled my love in your heart deep.
Your heart is open and sings with joy.
The love that we share is always with me.

Entry 9: 1997

Footsteps on the Floor

Now my dad—he was a big guy; a strong guy. When it came to taking care of me, he wasn't quite sure of all the right moves. He was a bit awkward in that department, but that didn't bother me one bit. I could feel his fierce and deep love for me. Whenever he would look at me, I could sense that he was moved on a very deep level and knew it was awesome that I had made it into his life and his presence.

I couldn't see very well, but I could sense my dad's presence more than I could see him. I knew his scent and the vibration of his footsteps when he came close to me. I could see that his heart was big and strong and that he was filled with a powerful love for me. I looked forward to his comings and goings.

Dad looked after my mom and me. He kept the wheels

turning, so to speak. He was the spoke in the wheel that kept things rolling in the outside world. Meanwhile, my mother and I dealt with my little world. Sometimes it was hard for me to let Dad know how much I loved him. My appreciation for him was one hundred percent. How can I say it? All I could do was smile inside and hope that he could read my inner smile.

Dad
My dad is tall,
Way bigger than me.
Sets his smile upon me.
Precious baby boy,
He says to me.
You are mine
And always will be.

Entry 10: 1999

Charlie: Dream Girl and My Younger Sister

Then there is my sister, Charlie, who's not much younger than me; she was born two-and-a-half years after I was. I didn't think my parents would have another child after my traumatic birth—who knew? What a doll baby for a sister! Oh man, Charlie was everyone's dream girl.

Charlie is a beauty in all ways. She has an open heart, she has a good attitude, and she makes friends easily. These are just a few of her attributes. After she was born, I had some competition; she was the cutest baby now. I didn't take to that so well at first. Because of the appearance of Charlie on the scene, I had some readjusting to do. I still had lots to mull over in my mind about this sudden change of events. Before too long though, she had charmed me completely. I made room for her in my heart; she wasn't too bad. She could do things that I might never do. She could walk. A walking baby girl that looked like a miracle to me. Sometimes she would run into my room and caress my arm as if I were her personal baby doll; she had such a sweet air about her. She was mysterious, ragged, and wild.

I could tell that she was a happy girl because of her touch. Soon this baby doll learned how to talk, so she could actually tell me how much she loved me. Charlie whispered things in my ear that she might never remember, but I remember everything she said–all of them, Charlie. I wanted to tell her how much I loved her, but I couldn't say a word; I can only reminisce about all the things I wanted to express. Charlie, I want to speak to you in the way I am now, through my journal; I want to tell you how much I love you. All the times we spent together are special to me and I cherish them. My baby sister, my only sister! We were young then, just babies. My love always, sister!

P.S. I have a vague memory of a pumpkin Charlie, do you know about that?

Charlie

My sister is a part of me,
Her energy streams all around me.
Her beauty is like ribbons gold,
Dancing up and down with me.

Entry 11: 2002

Wild Rides with Brother Riley

Now I want to fill you in on the details of one other interesting family member. I want to tell you about my little brother, Riley. Basically, he's the youngest in the family. Riley had a way of making me laugh, he was like some kind of heavenly clown. It seemed he was born just to make me laugh. His eyes would sparkle and light up with mischief whenever he played with me. He never seemed to care that I might get upset by his playful moods. As I say, he was a born clown.

Riley liked to push me around in what I imagined to be my magic wheelchair. He would play around and make my chair go in circles, just as if we were dancing to-gether. His hair used to fly in the wind whenever we were outside playing together. Riley would laugh and laugh like crazy, and so would I. I laughed on the inside, he laughed on the outside.

Whenever we were at the beach, Riley would push me

around in the sand. Let me tell you something–that certainly was no easy task. Try pushing a heavy wheelchair around in the sand! That effort might take all your strength away. I love Riley so much!

We used to play with balloons. Riley would try and get a reaction from me by bouncing balloons off my body. I especially liked it when he would "accidentally" pop a balloon in hopes of startling me and making me laugh. I like to think he had a kind of dark sense of humor like me.

Sprite
Riley is way cool,
He knows how I rule.
He is a sprite,
With lots of might.
He whirls me and twirls me,
With his dancing moves.

Entry 12: 1997

Eating on the Run

The new doctor from New England was one of the first cutting-edge physicians that took a special interest in my case. He was one of my grandmother's doctors–I knew that he had been there for her throughout many years. On one occasion, I know he saved her life.

She felt that if anyone could help me, it would be this guy. He was an orthomolecular biochemist, and the patients he took on were ones that were considered to be total lost causes. These lost causes were the ones that the medical field would abandon and say, "nothing more could be done for this patient." The local hospitals would often send this doctor some patients that were in the process of dying; he was highly revered by the hospital doctors. He was the kind of man who was expected to pull off miracles, and he often did just that.

I was six months old when I first went to see this special doctor. He knew everything about my medical history. I stood on very fragile ground, and he knew best what my body needed to help rebuild itself, and for me to live. The specialist set up a specific procedure for me; it was planned for me and only me. It was a regimen consisting of certain supplements that would be nourishing to both my brain and body. Throughout the years, the supplement protocol would change. The vitamin supplements proved to be very beneficial.

★ ★ ★

My mom or Gum Gum would put some milk in a blender and blend the supplements with it or with food when it was time for me to be fed. I'm sure the mixed-up milk would have tasted horrible had I been forced to drink it by mouth because it smelled awful! I was lucky I didn't have to taste the supplements, as I was always fed through a feeding tube. My taste buds never had to go through that kind of trauma.

About the feeding tube–a small tube was inserted

through the outside of my belly, and on the inside of my belly was a balloon that kept the tube from falling out. This was how I enjoyed my meals. Although everything seemed fine, on several occasions the balloon broke. This was bad! It sent my family members running and scurrying about the place like rabbits in an open field, because that meant we had to go right to the children's hospital in Pittsburgh to get a new tube.

★ ★ ★

We went to New England often so that I could be monitored on a regular basis. Most of the time it was me, my mother, Gum Gum as the driver, Charlie, Riley, and my valets who went to see this great doctor. *I much prefer to say valets instead of nurses, it sounds more sophisticated; manlier for a guy like me. I want you to know I am not a baby. Some people think that individuals with disabilities need to be babied, but that is simply not true.*

★ ★ ★

Riley remembers going in the van with me. He often told me the trips to New England are the ones he cherishes the most. My mother would turn those trips into sweet vacations so that other family members could have some fun also. One of my most memorable trips was to a beach there. It's special to me because my dad, grandfather, Aunt Alex, and Uncle Bobby went too. My mother and grandmother rented little cottages on the beach. I had my own room in the tiny bungalow with my own proper valet and all the necessities that kept me alive and kicking, so to speak. You know the drill–suction machines with extra tubes, canned milk, oxygen tanks, wheelchair, and plenty of bibs, diapers, and clothes. I almost forgot, my poor Aunt Alex lost her 'explorer' wallet that Gum Gum bought for her, thinking it was the best thing ever. I felt bad for my aunt when she found the wallet...with no money in it. Not only had she lost her life savings, but now she was still stuck with that wallet that Grandma thought was so cool.

Entry 13: 2003

A Narrow Escape

My suction pump has a rechargeable battery that can run for short periods of time without being plugged in. Once the battery charge runs down, without being recharged, I'm in big trouble. I could quite literally choke to death on my own snot and spit. I could also swallow saliva into my lungs, causing aspiration pneumonia. So, you see why it is critical that the suction pump battery is always charged. In our adapted van, to keep it charged, the pump's battery is plugged into the cigarette lighter for the duration of our road trip. Once we arrive at our destination, the pump is plugged into an outlet.

Today we were driving to New Hampshire where the

orthomolecular biochemist sees patients. It wasn't until we were well on the road–I'd say eight hours in and too late to turn back–when the nurse said she couldn't find the wall charger. There wasn't much they could do until we arrived at the hotel.

Once at the hotel, all three of them–Mom, Gum Gum, and the nurse–franticly searched through all my bags looking for the wall charger. It was just not there; it had not been packed, and my suction pump was almost dead. Panic started to set in, but then Mom got an idea.

Gum Gum stayed with me while Mom hurriedly left to find a store that might carry something to charge my suction pump. This was in an unfamiliar city, which made it difficult for my mom to know where to look. After going to a variety of different stores, Mom found an electronics place that carried a power converter that the cigarette lighter end of the car charger could be plugged into. Time was of the essence in getting the power converter back to the hotel. Mom made it back to me just in time–the day was saved and so was I!

Funny how something so incidental and small is taken for granted. It can mean the difference between life and death! This is one of the few times I got into trouble in all my travels. The seriousness of the situation hit all of us. From then on, Gum Gum or Mom always checked my travel bags after the nurses packed them for me. My equipment necessities were checked one by one before we left my room.

P.S. Many years later…some other things were forgotten, but they weren't my belongings. My sister, Charlie, packed one pair of shorts, one dirty T-shirt, and nothing else in her bag for a two-week trip–Mom couldn't believe it. Ha! Ha!

Entry 14: 1999

Dive! Dive! Dive!

Today, I'm going diving with Gum Gum. We'll sit inside a hyperbaric oxygen chamber when we "dive." Mom and Gum Gum take turns diving with me. The hyperbaric chamber that Gum Gum and I are getting into resembles a giant bubble. Ever seen one of these things?

I haven't been in one like this before; usually the chamber is a long, round glass tube that's shaped much like a cigar. The hyperbaric oxygen chamber will push oxygen through my skin into all my cells. I am hoping that my drowsy and sleepy brain cells will suddenly get some new energy and wake up. If this were to happen, I know I would feel better.

A few doctors felt that I was just a vegetable and I would never be able to do anything that normal, healthy people do. My special pediatrician, along with other doctors, told my parents that it wasn't worth my having this hyperbaric treatment; it would not do me any good. "Hyperbaric oxygen therapy (HBOT) will simply have no effect. It's a waste of your time and money," they explained. Mom and Gum Gum did not take too kindly to their naysaying words. I am so grateful that they didn't listen to those negative doctors–I guess we will see who is right. Why is it that sometimes when moving forward, people have to feel they are going against the grain?

When we go for this treatment we're told not to wear lotion, cosmetics, perfumes, products, deodorants, or wigs (the mention of a wig always makes me laugh). Neither are we allowed to wear jewelry or contacts. This might be hard for Gum Gum because she uses some of those things. The people in charge of this special chamber need to be informed as to whether I am taking medications and what they are.

★★★

My grandma is all ready to "dive" with me; I guess she is ready for anything to happen. Whatever happens, she is all right with it. At least, that's what I think. She begins climbing down through a small porthole opening in the top of the chamber (we have to sit in this HBOT chamber).

Mom and the dive technician lift me up, fit me through the porthole, and hand me down to Gum Gum. She helps guide me down and sits me right in front of her, then holds me tight against her body. The hatch is being closed now and we are down inside this small explorer submarine-type bubble. We only have the little porthole to look through. It's best if I stay in this bubble for only one hour, but I wonder if anyone is holding a stopwatch and paying attention as the minutes tick by. This seems like a long time. Are we going to stay in our magic bubble forever?

I don't think Gum Gum is enjoying this experience in the chamber very much. I can sense her nervousness because of the way she is trying to make the most of each one of her breaths. Her breathing sounds weird, not like her normal self. I myself don't mind being confined in a small space; maybe that's because I'm about four years old and very small anyway. Nothing seems out of place for me.

★★★

We've only been in here for about ten or fifteen minutes and Gum Gum is definitely having a hard time. I think she is having a panic attack, or something like that. She is trying to act all grown up and control her panic and claustrophobia. Let's face it, she really doesn't like being confined or cooped up in this very small space. I know she wants out of this situation and she wants out fast! She's not going to make it for sure; nothing is going right for her. Ten minutes later–I knew this was going to happen–Gum Gum finally had to tell someone, "get me out of here! This is all too much for me. No more!"

Gum Gum is in full panic mode now. At that time, I felt really bad for her because I have never seen anything get the best of her. Crazy me, I also wanted to laugh (I wanted to laugh at her the same way she had wanted to laugh at me when I went into a crazy kind of madness on the beach. That's a story for another day). It's a strange feeling…having concern for someone while wanting to laugh and cry at the same time. I guess if you know they're okay, it is all right to laugh. Do you know the difference between good laughter and bad laughter? I've known both kinds, and the kind of laughter I am talking about here makes the angels laugh right along with me. I like to think so, anyway. I hope I'm not wrong.

★★★

The man in charge of the hyperbaric chamber is going through the process of shutting it down so Gum Gum can get out. She couldn't believe that she needed to get out. Yes, she quit. Grandma felt bad about not being able to stay in the chamber for the entire hour. This was her first time in this type of hyperbaric chamber; it was extremely small for two people and the feeling of being locked in only amplified the feeling of being confined.

Mom got in with me after Gum Gum climbed out. She seems perfectly fine in this small hyperbaric chamber. I am glad I have a second chance in the bubble; they are taking me down again. Yes, I am fully ready to enjoy this experience of my body soaking up every ounce of oxygen that's available.

I have had many other HBOT treatments before, but this dive feels to me a little different somehow. My head feels like something inside is starting to light up and sparkle. I notice two long, plump things that resemble clubs extending outward from either side of my torso— what is this I'm seeing? The plump club-like things extending out from my body feel tingly and move a little. A rush of ecstatic joy, mixed with the happiness of tears, suddenly coursed through my entire body. I tingled all over with this feeling.

In that moment, I knew that my mind had made a connection

of recognition that these clubs were really my arms. My mind now knew, and I knew, that these were arms and I could move them. This realization struck me so profoundly that my body shuddered from the feelings that surged through me—feelings that I never wanted to end—they were so empowering.

There is only one way to put that realization and what I felt into words... *"it felt like I had been touched by the hand of God, in a moment of timelessness that extended forever. I was completely and totally engulfed in this feeling. I was being healed by bits and pieces and most definitely was not a vegetable. I was aware, alive, and knew I had arms that could move—maybe not a whole lot, but I could use these funny looking things called arms."*

Entry 15: 2004

Where Am I Now?

I had a special chair—a wheelchair—that had four knobby tires, a custom molded back and seat, and two push handles. I like to think of it as a self-driving chair, much like a self-driving car. The only trouble was that my self-driving wheelchair sometimes took me to places that I didn't want to go. For instance, I would want to go outside on a nice sunny morning to feel the wind on my face, hear the birds sing, feel the sun shining on my body, and follow my siblings around. Instead, I would find myself going to school or going to the doctor's office at a children's hospital–ugh.

There were other times, though, that I'd find myself having a wonderful time in a new and interesting place, such as a zoo or an amusement park. It didn't take me long to realize that I clearly did not have control over my self-driving chair; it did what it wanted to do and when it wanted to do it without consulting me. I never knew where the heck I was going! Could it be someone else was in control of my special wheelchair?

Entry 16: 2004

Rental Vans and Airplanes

A turning point came in my life when I was seven years old. My mother had heard of a brain doctor that lived in Florida. She felt this brain doctor might be able to help me, so off we went on a new exciting adventure.

The vans that Mom rented did not have a ramp, and so I could not sit in my own seat; I was not very comfortable without the support of my special chair. Every time we drove somewhere in a rental van, my wheelchair had to be taken apart to fit inside. When we arrived at our destination, it had to be taken out of the van and put back together again.

At home I had a van that was made specially for me; I was much more comfortable when I could actually sit in my own wheelchair. My grandmother was usually the driver in my adapted adventure vehicle, or whatever Mom could rent when traveling. In my souped-up van an automatic ramp came down with a push of a button. At that point, I would be rolled in. To secure my wheelchair, all four sides were strapped down to the floor.

Once I was secured in place, we were ready to go anywhere we wanted. My mother, brother, sister, and valets would go too. We always took a valet—or two—because we needed to; and we felt they might enjoy the journey with us.

This trip, however, we didn't drive my adapted van. We flew in an airplane to Florida, and Mom rented a minivan at the Tampa airport.

Ready to Fly
I'm on the plane all settled in,
Waiting for the rev-up to begin.
I'm looking out the window now,
At sunlit clouds and sky of blue.
Telling me, it's time to move.

Entry 17: 2004

Thinking Outside of the Box

Tomorrow is my appointment with the brain doctor in Florida; excitement exists all around us. I got caught up in it too. It was contagious, and I couldn't help myself. I didn't know what to expect or not to expect from this guy. I had been to many doctors throughout the years and had always expected a change every time. There were a couple of doctors that found me interesting, but for the most part, it always led to a disappointing dead-end. What was going to happen this time?

My mom and grandmother were always looking for cutting-edge practitioners who tried things way outside out of the box. They were looking for miracle workers who had new ways to help people like me. Maybe there were some doctors out there who might get a kick out of me and decide to go beyond the everyday "grocery store" products the medical field usually offered.

Entry 18: 2004

Magic Cream

Today is my first appointment at the new neurologist's office, so I was being especially alert. I didn't want to miss anything. I still remember driving into the doctor's parking lot; his office was in an old white house on a back street in town. We (my entourage and I) unloaded and went inside. It was curious how we all became very quiet. Once inside, we were afraid to be excited and hopeful, for fear that this wouldn't be any different than the other treatments we had tried. So, we were quietly holding our breath in silent prayer.

I do know though that my parents and grandparents always held a powerful faith in their hearts of a miracle coming my way. There also was a fear that if the words of a miracle were spoken out loud, it would be jinxed. The word miracle is a big word if let loose or spoken aloud; it could cause pain if it backfired, so it was best to keep such a big word close to one's heart.

It's my turn to see the doctor. The three of us–Mom, Grandma, and I–all went into his office. The doctor explained what he felt was the best approach to begin with for my case. He described how some of the cells in my brain might be dormant or asleep, and needed to be awakened. He said that if we could get more oxygen to my brain, some of the dormant cells might wake up and give me a new lease on life. The neurologist took a tube of topical ointment out of his white doctor's jacket; he called it nitroglycerin. Next, he very gently rubbed one very small dot of nitroglycerin on my arm and told us to come back the next day.

None of us saw any noticeable difference after I experienced my first treatment. I don't know what I was expecting, but I was expecting something magical. Throughout the years, we had certainly learned not to get our hopes up too much, but this particular doctor's visit seemed to have a different feel to it. I admit, I had high hopes and I thought something miraculous was about to happen; I'm disappointed. I know my mom and grandma are disappointed too.

Entry 19: 2004

A Turning Point

The next day, we returned to the doctor's office for the second time. The neurologist pulled out the same tube of paste from his pocket and smoothed the nitroglycerin on my arm again. After he put the ointment on me, we were told to wait a few minutes; then he said to come back tomorrow. He was waiting for a reaction from me in some noticeable way, but the same thing happened as the day before. What a big deal...nothing was happening, absolutely nothing!

The following day we all went back again–third time's a charm. The neurologist pulled out the same tube of nitroglycerin cream from his jacket pocket and rubbed two spots on my arm this time instead of just one. After the disappointment of the last two days, I never thought anything exciting would ever happen.

Again, we were told to wait in a room. While doing so, Mom put a napkin on my head and covered my face to calm me down. She often did this to block out lights and sounds when I got overstimulated. She slowly removed the cloth napkin, as though she was playing a game of peek-a-boo with me. Suddenly, the unexpected happened...

Slowly, I began to feel my face and lips start to move, quiver, and shift. The feeling inside me was warm and good; this was something I had never experienced before. I felt a happiness flow through me–this was a new sensation; so new that I didn't know the proper or right name for this feeling.

I felt like kicking my legs because of this new way I was feeling. I realized my lips had widened and turned up on the sides, I think my teeth were even showing. What was happening to me? My face began to come alive; it felt different. This was the strangest feeling I could ever have imagined. It was kind of scary at first, but it felt good at the same time. While I was experiencing this new shift in myself, my mother and grandmother stood in front of me. I sensed that they were in awe and unable to speak.

They were overcome with a joy that brought tears to their eyes, tears that had not been there before. Deep tears that came from the depth of their souls. An unbelievable thing had just occurred, a miracle had happened, and they were there to witness and share in it with me. I was seven years old, and my life changed forever! I was transformed!

Entry 20: 2004

Miracle Child

Then I knew…I was smiling; smiling for the first time in seven years! THIS WAS MY MIRACLE! MY MIRACLE! The miracle we had waited for, the miracle everyone had prayed for all those years! The neurologist gave my family and me the greatest gift ever.

I had a miracle and now I could smile to convey my love and happiness, I could use my smile to talk and interact with my family and valets. It's hard to put into words the happiness that this change brought to me and my family. It quite literally changed all our lives in unimaginable ways.

To add to the miracle, two weeks later I began laughing out loud while rambunctiously kicking my legs and waving my arms. These were all things that I had never done before either. This miracle was mine; it was the start of a new life, a new chapter, for my family and me.

I can't help but say it over again—this touched all our hearts and souls on such a deep level. Even after all these years, the event never ceases to amaze me and stir me inside with love, thankfulness, and tears. In just one day, seven years were completely erased; I was transformed, and could now live a much fuller life with my family.

Come Play with Me
No boundaries can hold me,
My love flows free.

My soul screams out,
Come play with me.
Let's share our love
For what is to be.
Sing songs of gladness for fruitful trees.
Tell me now of your crosses,
We will take them off,
So you can be set free,
To come play with me.

Entry 21: 2004

Vow of Silence

It was a miracle for me because for seven years I never smiled. My family never knew what I felt, except for the pain I experienced. They often wondered about whether I could see or hear because I didn't show any expression in any way, shape, or form. Sometimes it was hard for my family that I couldn't show any expressions of love, happiness, or recognition. I could sense the traces of discouragement and the question of, "would this ever change?" Those feelings didn't last long, though; my family was amazingly resilient, and inner strength was their gift.

I never told them that I did know who they were. I knew each one by scent and smell, the sound and tone of their voice, and movements that had a vibrational quality to them. I recognized them by the way I was being held, the kind of kisses each one would give me and where they would kiss me. I knew the way in which someone dressed me or gave me a shower, how I was being fed, or who gave me vitamins, and the way someone would touch me or run their fingers through my hair (I liked that a lot).

I knew who played my audio tapes or music by the choices that they made. It was amusing sometimes when my valets would put something on that I didn't like. When that happened, I would kick up a fuss. Everyone had their favorites that they felt were mine too. Clearly, some CDs were not my favorites, especially baby stuff. I was an older boy now and I wanted big boy books read to me, and big boy music and audio stories to listen to. My mother always knew when it was time to buy me new audio books and music that reflected my age—she had a sense about that kind of thing.

Entry 22: 2004

Fire Trucks and Flashing Lights

It was our third trip to see the doctor in Florida. It was ten in the morning and already a humid ninety-five degrees.

After my doctor's appointment, my mother and grandmother loaded us kids in the van. Grandma was always the driver/chauffeur on these trips. Well, before loading up us kids, she threw the keys on the driver's seat and shut the door so her hands would be free.

That was the start of all that happened. My mother went to get in the van, since we were all loaded now, except for her and Grandma. She couldn't get in because her door was locked, so Mom asked my grandmother to unlock her door. Gum Gum was still standing outside the van, and when she went to get in, her door was locked too. At the same time, they both realized that when Grandma threw the keys on the driver's seat and closed her door, all the van doors had accidentally locked somehow. My brother was a toddler and my sister was about four years old, so no one inside the van was old enough to unbuckle and unlock the doors. Extreme panic hit Mom and Grandma. How were they going to get us out of the van quickly?

My mother called 911 and explained the situation. Very soon after that we heard sirens from police cars and fire trucks; we saw flashing lights of many colors. There was an awesome parade coming down the street! A few minutes later, all the fire trucks and police cars pulled into the doctor's parking lot.

We kids soon realized that there was no parade, no fire, and no crime; they were all coming to help us. We were the ones that were in distress—our van was parked in the sweltering sun and the temperature was rising. The parade of vehicles was coming in full force to rescue three children, and a handicapped kid at that; one who could choke at anytime. The firemen and policemen came so quickly that we didn't think they were for us. In truth, my siblings and I were calm throughout the whole ordeal. We just gazed on at the sound and light entertainment, wondering what the panic was all about.

My grandmother and I looked through the window at each other. She could understand by the look on my face what I was trying to convey to her—I was calm, and so were Charlie and Riley. All three of us were sitting inside the van, nonchalantly watching the men who wore red hats and blue uniforms. Even though Gum Gum understood the possible dire consequences of the situation, she didn't show any signs of fear. In the end, the police officers very quickly slid a special tool down inside the window and unlocked all the doors. We were saved!

I wonder if our story made the evening news.

Entry 23: 2005

Swimming with Dolphins

This time when we went to see my doctor in Florida, a dolphin excursion was planned for me. Mom and Gum Gum had heard wonderful things about the ability of dolphins to sense certain people and give them a healing boost of sorts. We were all excited.

Everyone was going—Mom, Grandma, Charlie, Riley, and my valet. None of us had ever swam with dolphins before. There was a pontoon boat waiting for us at the dock, it was time to go out on the ocean. There wasn't too much difficulty getting me and everyone else on board the float boat.

We left shore and headed out to find wild dolphins. A group of them were located, so we anchored nearby. I was already wearing a life vest, but a second life jacket was wrapped around my front. I also had a buoy-type thing around me to ensure that my head could not move forward or backward, and that I wouldn't be able to roll over or slide out of any of the life jackets.

I had two professional instructors, my valet, my mom, and Gum Gum to help me float in the water. This was a complicated endeavor, so we needed all hands on deck. I was helped into the water as gracefully as possible, under the circumstances of having all this gear on. Boy, was I a sight. I was enchanted by the feeling of the salt water, as it not only glides over me but pushes against my body. It's as if I'm being rocked and lovingly embraced by the sea.

Slowly, the dolphins started coming up to me. One touched my toes and I felt soft, electric shocks of pleasure move up through my toes and feet that made me feel alive in a wonderful, new, unusual way. I exploded in laughter and began kicking and waving my arms as much as I could; my helpers had a hard time holding onto me. I went wild and just couldn't contain myself after the dolphin touched my foot.

★★★

We went on a second dolphin excursion. On this trip, however, the water was rougher and dirtier, and there were too many jellyfish for my liking. Gum Gum was sitting with her legs hanging off the back of the pontoon boat, and as her feet were in the water, a couple dolphins swam up to her. She yelled for my mom to come and put her feet in the water too. Soon we were all in the water, hoping this trip would be as successful as the first one.

Dolphins
Dolphins nibble at my toes,
Playful action upon me.
Shivers delight through me,
Laughing, kicking it sends me.
Rollicking fun in an ocean breeze.

Entry 24: 2005

Sand Key Parrot

On one of our other trips to see the doctor in Florida, we stayed on Sand Key Island. I really liked staying at that place, but there was one thing that bothered me...in the hotel lobby stood a huge bird cage with a talking, squawking parrot sitting on a branch.

My brother Riley loved this big, colorful bird named Lisa. Every time we walked into the hotel, Riley would run up to the parrot and try to make her talk. My sister, Charlie, would then follow suit and join Riley in this craziness to get the bird to speak. I endured this bothersome ritual every day for about ten minutes; and at least once a day, if not two or three times in a day.

★★★

Oh no! Now I'm being pushed towards the cage to admire this parrot that I think is stupid and annoying. I clearly do not share the same affinity for birds that Riley does; I do not want to be bothered with the parrot.

★★★

Towards the end of our stay, I became more tolerant of Lisa and her squawking noises. The reason for the change was that I watched Riley run up to the bird and saw the immense delight it gave him, and I slowly started to enjoy watching Riley instead of the parrot. I no longer heard the squawking bird or felt annoyed by its presence. I now felt his joy and love for the parrot; I was feeling through Riley, and I could share in his merriment.

Lisa
Pretty parrot on a swing,
Doing nothing, but squawking.
I can hear you loud and clear.
Please, just shut your beak for me.

Entry 25: 2007

Lights, Camera, Sound, Action!

Mom and Gum Gum would always try to think of ideas for where they could take me that I might enjoy. One time, Gum Gum cooked up a plan to take me to the movies; her thinking was that the screen was so big, I might be able to see it.

One day, we all got together and chose the best time for me to watch a movie. We wanted it to be when the movie theater was least busy. You see, I could be quite noisy with my suction pump, coughing, and laughing, and we didn't want to disturb the other moviegoers.

When the day finally came, we loaded up the van with everyone. No one wanted to miss this adventure! With Gum Gum in the driver's seat, we went to the movies. This theater lobby was big and filled with people milling around. All the people were talking and laughing as they carried bags of popcorn and drink cups in their hands (although the popcorn and drinks were unknown objects to me because my eyesight was poor).

Mom was off buying the tickets while I was trying to take in this new place filled with fun and unfamiliar smells. The theater hallway was long, dark, and narrow; I was enthralled–it was like being in another world, a world of mysterious surprises (I like surprises).

I was positioned in a spacious area near the front of the movie screen (I always get VIP). All my equipment was organized and made ready for use in case I needed anything. I sat there waiting, for I had no concept of what a movie theater even was. Suddenly, there was an explosion of colors, lights, sounds, and action on the gigantic screen in front of me.

My eyes got big, my back tried to straighten, and I didn't make a sound; I forgot about the uncooperative ways of and pain in my body. I was spellbound in a magical land outside of myself. I started to feel that smile, where my teeth show, spread across my face.

I went wild inside with excitement! This was what a movie was! I loved it! Yes, I was a little noisy—laughing and all—but no one was bothered by it. This was the best idea yet.

The movie experience was a success! My mother saw how much I fancied this encounter, so she bought me a seventy-two-inch television to watch at home.

After that day, we went to the movies a few other times, and once to the IMAX theater (the IMAX movie blew my mind).

Entry 26: 2008

Riding the Dragon

I marveled at the ingenuity of my family and the lengths to which they went to find ways for me to enjoy life with them. My family members involved me in every aspect of their lives; I did everything and went everywhere they could take me. Even though I needed around the clock care, timed medicines, and feedings, they found a way to do fun things with me.

Sometimes in the summer, my family would take me to a small amusement park where I was able to ride the rides with one of them. One of my favorite rides (second to the rollercoaster) was called the *Sea Dragon*. This ship had dragon heads on it and swung back and forth, making a wide arc high up into the air.

Usually, Mom or Dad rode the dragon ride with me, but this time Grandma decided to get onboard with me. There were no seatbelts, so she tightly wrapped her arms around me. Once the ride was in full swing, Grandma had a lot of trouble holding on to me. I kept sliding off the seat and under the grab bar every time the ship swung high. Of course, I was laughing hysterically, but Grandma was scared and nervous that she would lose her grip on me and I would fall off the ride. After that, she refused to take me on the dragon ride again; she didn't want anyone else to take me on it either. I guess Gum Gum didn't want to lose me to the dragon.

★★★

My decision to come here and put trust in my family far exceeded any expectations I might have had. They could have very easily gone another direction and chosen to not participate in this play where they were the supporting actors. They never complained about their roles. They never quit on me!

Whirly Twirly
Way high up on the ride,
I look down upon the crowd.
Little ants they look to be,
As I whirl and twirl freely.

Entry 27: 2005

Going to School

I loved school. I had a lot of school friends. We would go on field trips to the fire station, Lake Erie, and to the zoo. We also enjoyed interesting and fun classroom parties.

★★★

One time, a man brought his donkey to school and I got to pet it. His coat felt soft, but maybe this was because it was a baby donkey. He made a noise when I touched him—that was pretty cool. Another time, someone brought in a puppy and it licked my face; I'm not so sure that I liked that slobber smeared all over my face.

★★★

We did all kinds of crazy things. One Christmas party, the teacher's aide put earrings on me; one was a gingerbread man, and the other one was a Christmas tree. The earrings were really big–they went down past my shoulders. I looked pretty goofy and my friends and I laughed at the mere sight of me. We also made headdresses that looked like bunny ears, frogs, antlers, or whatever we had in mind to make. We laughed hysterically at each other when we wore our silly headdresses.

★★★

I liked reading time at school. In fact, a nurse kept a monthly log of all the books that she read to me. One month, there were forty-one books on my reading list. I don't know where the nurse found the time to read so many books to me, because between the two of us we were always busy causing trouble (fun trouble, of course). I painted, drew, and made lots of things with my nurse.

★★★

I certainly didn't like it much when I was sick and had to stay home from school. But, I wouldn't like it if I made my classmates sick either.

Entry 28: 2012

Kitty's Treat: The Pinky Finger

A short yellow school bus came to my house every weekday to pick me and the nurse up and take us to school. The bus had a hydraulic lift that rose up and down so my wheelchair and I could easily be loaded onto it.

On this particular day, we had a very memorable and unexpected incident, to say the least. The nurse and I were waiting outside when the short yellow bus pulled up for us. The curly-haired bus driver got out and proceeded to lower the automatic hydraulic lift for my wheelchair. In doing so, the woman somehow caught her little finger in the ramp. The tip of her pinky finger was cut off!

At this point, it all went bad for the curly-haired bus driver. She started getting dizzy and feeling queasy and faint. The nurse and I helped the bus driver into my entryway. The night nurse was still inside doing her paperwork, so now both of them tended to the injured bus driver.

My mother came to say goodbye to me and found me sitting all alone in my bedroom. Mom wasn't too happy about finding me alone and wondered what was going on. The day nurse quickly explained to Mom what had happened to the bus driver while the night nurse called the bus company and the ambulance.

Apparently, fingers can be sewn back on, so before the ambulance came, my mother and the day nurse went outside to look for the severed pinky finger. They noticed the driver had painted her finger nails with a pink polish, so Mom and the nurse were hoping that the pink nail polish on the fingernail would jump out at them and they would find the severed fingertip much easier. They did not, however, find the pinky finger with the pink polish on it.

The EMTs arrived; they put the faint bus driver on a cart and wheeled her into the ambulance. Off they went. I assume they took the dizzy bus driver to the hospital.

My grandmother came into my room just in time to see the tail end of all the chaos that was happening–the search for the pink-painted pinky finger and the bus driver being carted outside to the ambulance. She didn't seem much concerned, but it takes a lot to get Grandma pulled into any kind of drama. She just couldn't understand how something like that could have happened when the lift was automatic.

Later, my dad came home from work. As Dad was driving up the driveway, he saw our cat, Cameron, flicking something around in his mouth and acting strange. Dad thought what the cat was doing was odd but didn't think any more about it. At dinner, Dad told my family how he saw the cat trying to chew on something and how strange Cameron's behavior seemed to him.

My mom patiently listened to my dad's story. After he was finished, she told him about the morning incident with the curly-haired bus driver losing the tip of her pinky finger with pink polish to the bus lift.

At the same time, both of my parents realized Cameron was the one who had found the pinky fingertip with the pink nail polish on it and thought it was a tasty kitty treat.

My mom and dad could not contain their laughter as they envisioned Cameron off enjoying his find.

Kitty's Treat
Tip of finger pink,
Is the kitty's treat.
Accidental find,
On the nurses' beat.
Emergency at best,
Driver's accident.

Entry 29: 2010

Star Athlete

I participated in the Special Olympics. I really didn't enjoy it much in the early years; most of my brain cells were either dead or dormant and I didn't know what the heck was going on around me. I think my nurse was entering the games, competing in them, and saying it was me.

After my miracle when I was seven, I went into the Special Olympics with a new attitude; my school friends and I all signed up. I was excited and got carried away by the prospect of showing off my talent and skill, and maybe winning a ribbon or two.

The Special Olympics were held at our local fairgrounds and Gum Gum came to watch me play in the games. I entered the softball throwing contest and the wheelchair races. I have my sunglasses and visor on, I am ready. I anxiously await my turn with my nurse and hope that she is into winning as much as I am, since this is the first time I actually have enough brain cells to participate. It's my turn now for the ball throwing contest. I have the biggest grin on my face that you can imagine. I don't know how I'm going to throw the ball because I'm laughing so hard. I muster up all my arm strength and the nurse helps me lift my arm high. Off the ball goes–high and long.

"I won! I won! I won a blue ribbon!"

Next comes the wheelchair race. We are all lined up now, waiting for the start. BANG! We're off and running, and I can hear Gum Gum and mom cheering me on. I'm making all kinds of noise–laughing hysterically and kicking my legs– encouraging the nurse to run faster, faster, so I could win the race.

WOW! This has been the best fun ever! All my friends won races too, ribbons were presented all around. The ribbons and all the activities made it a very happy day for all of us.

Entry 30:1998

My Special Horse

Grandma gave me a stuffed horse when I was a little boy. The plush horse was mostly dark brown with white and black markings on his face and body. *The horse you gave me was bigger than I was when you gave it to me, Gum Gum.*

My grandma would have it jump around me, trying to get me to like it. Sometimes when I would wake up from a nap, the first thing I would see was this horse. Grandma had come in while I was sleeping and put it under my arm, so my hand would be resting on it. The way she took it everywhere I went…I think she loved this horse more than I did.

As I grew older, the horse was one of the things that became very special to me; I had it on my bed all the time. And if it wasn't there on my bed, Gum Gum would put it there. When I got to be a lot bigger than the horse, some people thought that I was too old to enjoy it anymore. That wasn't true, of course; but that didn't stop that someone from moving the stuffed animal into another room. Gum Gum would eventually notice that I didn't have my horse, though; she'd go find it and bring it back to give it to me.

★★★

After I passed away, a cute little blonde girl came to our house. When the little girl saw my horse, she wanted to take it home with her. My Gum Gum would have liked to give the stuffed toy to her, but she just could not part with this special horse that had once been mine and hers for so many years—it was an important part of our lives. Gum Gum wasn't ready to let go of the horse. For her, it was like saying goodbye to me if she gave it away, and that was not an option for her.

The little girl's mother, Sheila, found and bought a little stuffed horse that looked just like mine; it was just the right size for her. She showed it to my grandma the next time she visited. Gum Gum was surprised at the striking resemblance it had to my horse. Gum Gum was happy that the little girl now had her own special horse to play with, and no longer felt bad about keeping mine.

★★★

To this day, Gum Gum still has my horse in her room—it's on her bed now. When she looks at it she sees me, and perhaps she even feels me.

Entry 31: 2009

Staircase Surfing

The other day, while I was sitting in my bedroom, I saw Charlie and Riley running into my supply closet where all my diapers are kept. I saw them leave with their arms full of my diaper packages. Shortly after that, they ran back into the closet and did the same thing. They were carrying armfuls of my diapers–they were undoubtedly raiding my supplies. They did this many times; my diapers were disappearing at an alarming rate! I wouldn't have any left if they kept stealing them. They appeared to be very excited about something though. The nurse didn't even question their strange behavior. I don't know why, maybe it was because she was new.

What happened next was an unexpected surprise. My dad came in my room, scooped me up in his arms, and took me to the staircase. There, I saw the diaper packages all piled up at the bottom of the steps.

My dad stepped over the diapers and carried me up to the top of the stairs, and at the top was a mattress. With me in his arms, Dad sat down on the mattress. Hanging on to me tightly, he pushed off the landing, and down the steps we flew.

I was surfing, riding on a rollercoaster, and flying at the same time. I was sweaty from laughing so hard, and it was such fun I didn't want to stop. I took turns with Charlie and Riley. They could mattress surf all by themselves, of course. Since mattress surfing was their idea, I didn't mind taking turns.

★★★

The diapers my brother and sister stole were used as a crash pad for the mattress. As soon as my dad caught on to the diaper runs, and what Charlie and Riley were planning, he joined in on the fun and included me too. It made my day, which otherwise would have been uneventful and long.

Sled Ride
Down we fly,
Laughing hard with joy.
Up the steps to the top,
Surfing down, wanting more.

Entry 32: 2007

Hoofbeats and Horse Hair

I hear a soft-weighted, rhythmic *thug thug thug thug.* I didn't know what I was hearing (I later learn that the sound of hooves is the first thing I heard). Mom found a new therapy called hippotherapy. I soon found out that I am about to ride a horse for the first time.

Gum Gum and Mom unload me from my adapted van and wheel me into a big building. The smells are different, and it takes me some time to separate them from each other; they all kind of melded together. The smells are both pungent and friendly at the same time. Manure, hay, sawdust, and horse is what I finally distinguish.

There is talking going on all around me. Suddenly, Gum Gum pushes me up a long, wooden ramp and onto a platform. What is she doing? She is pushing me to the edge of the platform. I'm uneasy; this seems just a little too close. I do not like this feeling at all. Just think about it…here I am, high up at the edge of a platform, with no control over my wheelchair or myself. If I should go spastic–which I often do when I'm scared or happy–there is no telling what could happen. I am strong as a boy bull, I could break free of my straps and bindings, and off the edge I would go.

Now someone has brought a very large animal in front of me. I am told this gigantic and fierce looking animal is called a horse. This seems a bit sketchy to me and I'm not comfortable with this at all. Nervous and jittery are the best words for how I am feeling right now. As I come face to face with this thing called horse, I don't know what to expect. This is something new, and I hope I am going to like whatever this is all about.

Now all my straps and bindings are being taken off. I am hoisted onto the beast, and a therapist sits on horse to help me get situated comfortably. My hips and back are twisted and curved, so I can't sit in the normal position that one uses when riding horseback. Something is wrapped around me and the woman on horse; she has to be able to hold me and pin me to her body.

Oh boy, we are starting to move! I feel horse moving under me; it is a strange feeling. Something alive is moving under me with a steady movement, while I feel awkward and unsteady.

My hand falls down and touches this horse, and it feels like silky paintbrush hairs–soft, yet firm. As my hand feels the horse, I start to sense other things about the animal. I feel its leg movements, hear the snort of its breath, and hear its tail swishing. Without realizing it, I become aware that I am feeling different—a good different. I felt in tune with the rhythm of the horse, as if I am one with him. This was an amazing feeling!

Slowly throughout the session, I grew more and more comfortable with riding a horse. I learned to enjoy and look forward to my horse therapy. The movement of trotting is what I like the most—bouncing up and down makes me laugh like crazy.

★★★

There finally came a time when I was too big; the curvature of my back and hips made it too difficult for someone to hold me on the horse—I had to stop with the therapy.

Entry 33: 2008

Who is the Puppet Master?

I was a skinny boy with bent arms, legs, back, hands, feet, and nose. No, I didn't have a bent nose, I was being funny there. But, I did have the bentness in all my bones except for my toes, which were very nice toes; well-formed toes that were easy on the eyes.

My bones could become achingly painful, much like a door or window expanding or contracting, and my muscles would go into spasms that threw me around like a crazy boy. I felt like a puppet–where was that unknown person pulling the strings and making my body go into contorted weird movements and positions? I want to cut the strings and stop the shenanigans that are controlling me.

It doesn't really matter what season it was either; it was all year, day in, day out. Although, when the summer months were nice, my bones did feel better; they felt as if they were dried out and happy. Still bent, but happy. In the winter time, though...sodden, heavy, cold, and damp was how my bones felt.

Entry 34: 2008

I'm A Superhero

Every day I have splints and braces put on me. I have a set of both soft and hard hand splints, plus a set of hard ankle and foot braces. The hard plastic hand splints go up to my elbows and are put on when I sleep, while the soft neoprene ones are worn during the day. My ankle and foot braces are hard plastic too and are put on over my heels and calves; they stop below my knee. A full body brace goes around my torso and is buckled up in the back, and as if that wasn't enough, there is also a soft neck brace.

When my hard gear is on I am Luke Skywalker, superhero, fighting the crime of my body. The splints are supposed to help keep my limbs and body from completely curling in on itself. The hard gear is put on in the evenings and stays on throughout the night.

When morning comes, and I am showered and dressed, I model the soft hand splints and the rest of the gear for the day. Some days I get a break from the splints—mostly when I'm on vacation or traveling. These soft hand splints aren't as effective as the hard ones, but I can't be a superhero all the time, or can I?

I can be anything I want. My soft braces are seriously red, and they cover enough of my body that I do look like Spider-Man when I have them on. That's it—I am Spider-Man by day, and Luke Skywalker by night; a powerful force to contend with.

At the end of the day, when my grandmother would take the soft hand splints off me, my hands were stuck in a clenched fist; my grandmother needed to take the time to uncurl it. After my hand was open, she used a special soap to wash the palms of my hands and fingers. Gum Gum said that was the only soap that would take the smell away from the brutal combination of perspiration and the neoprene braces.

Now, my Gum Gum was funny about this; she kept washing my hands and smelling them until she was satisfied that the foul odor was gone and that I smelled good.

Entry 35: 2002

Torture Rack

There was a tall, rectangular piece of wood with wheels on it called a "stander" in my bedroom. This tall piece of wood was positioned upright and was meant for me to be stood up on or maybe even stretched a bit–that's how I felt about it, anyway. The purpose of this contraption was to put me in a weight-bearing position; a stance that was different than my everyday position of sitting in my wheelchair or lying in my bed. It looked rather like a tortuous thing to someone who didn't know what it was.

★★★

On this particular day, I saw the nurse pushing the stander into the middle of the room and I knew what that meant. It meant that I was going on the board today, and I didn't like it one bit. I watched her pivot the stander horizontally and lower it until it was waist-height.

I was hoping that she would be distracted by something else and forget about me. Then it occurred to me, if I pretend to be upset or start making all kinds of noise, maybe she would say, "oh, poor boy, he's too distressed; I won't put him on the rack today." Just then my mother came into the room and I knew immediately that I wouldn't get away with it. She could tell the difference between what was put on and what was for real.

Mom and the nurse came toward my bed with a look

79

of, "we're doing this," in their eyes. They picked me up and laid me down on the tall wooden plank. My feet were slid into the black footrest, and then I felt the straps going over my shins. Then came the straps that went over my legs and torso; they were buckled down the same as before. I am strapped onto the board now. Adjustments are made to the straps so hopefully I wouldn't be uncomfortable. Mom slowly raises the stander into an almost upright position, just enough that my head doesn't fall forward. I'll stay in that position until my time is up, or I became too uncomfortable and fuss. It all depends on how I am feeling today as to how long I stay standing.

★★★

There were times when I felt like I was living in the Middle Ages and waiting to be pardoned and taken off the rack.

Entry 36: 2009

Cadillac Journeys

I had a standard child-sized wheelchair when I was young. As I grew, I would get a different chair that suited my size and shape better. When I was about twelve years old, the curvature of my spine was approximately a sixty-five degree angle, so I needed a new, unique wheelchair. Mom and Gum Gum took me to an equipment place that made special form-fitted wheelchairs to accommodate such curvatures of the spine.

At the consultation I was laid down on a table and a cast was made of my back and spine. After the technicians were done making the cast, I was put back into my old wheelchair and loaded up in my adapted van. Grandma drove us back home.

★★★

Some weeks later, the day finally came...my custom-made wheelchair was ready for me; we drove back up to the equipment place to pick it up.

When I saw my new wheelchair, it was even more tricked out than I originally thought it was going to be. My new mobile lounger had a molded back and a gel cushioned seat so that I wouldn't get sores on my back or butt from sitting too long.

There were special features put on my new wheelchair too. The chair itself could be tilted back so I could sleep and rest more comfortably–it was like being in a lounge chair–if I had to sit in it for long periods of time. There was a custom metal shelf underneath the seat for my suction pump, and a bag for medicines and all my paraphernalia, so to speak.

The wheelchair had manual brakes on the handles, big knobby tires that were made for off-road pushing, footrests with foot straps to go over my shoes, and an adjustable head strap that went across my forehead to keep my head from falling forward or rolling around. This head strap meant that I didn't have to wear the neck collar that was so hot and uncomfortable anymore.

There was what mom called a butterfly harness that crisscrossed my chest, went up over my shoulders, and around my waist; this kept my torso from falling forward. My entire chair was made of breathable materials.

This new wheelchair of my mine was tricked out for sure, the only thing missing were some chrome wheels. I was so excited and wanted to get in this new means of transportation that I put up a fuss. It worked, and shortly after making a commotion, I was put in my new custom-fit wheelchair. WOW! What a difference from my old, rickety wheelchair. I was sitting in the Cadillac of rides.

A few adjustments were made for my comfort and I was ready to go. One last thing...once these adjustments had been made, no one–and I mean no one–was allowed to make any changes except my mom or grandma. If someone did, there was big trouble, with a capital T.

Dad gave Mom a special tool to adjust my headrest, and I saw her hide it from the nurses. She wasn't taking any chances of someone messing with my Cadillac.

Entry 37: 2009

The Star of the Show

Sometimes I would lie in my bed and wonder, "why am I here?" Eventually, I would remember why I agreed to come into this world in the way that I did. Before I was born, I saw the grand plan that was laid out for my family and me. I saw where I was going, and why I was going there.

Even with this knowledge, the choice to be made wasn't an easy one. If I accepted this mission...I knew it may not work and that I could die in the process of coming into the world; or that if I survived, I would be a prisoner of pain held captive inside a crippled body my entire life. It meant that I would need to have faith and put full trust in the people that would be my caretakers to fulfill their roles in this grand play in which I would have the starring role. Making the right choices—for all involved—would be an awesome feat to pull off. But could it be done if I couldn't speak? Would my family be able to "hear" me with their hearts?

This endeavor required a trust and strength so strong that nothing could break our bond. Everyone had to stand together as one in this if it was going to work. I struggled with my fears; I thought of all the possible ways this could go wrong. I knew that the people in my life would be fierce, I trusted that, but it still wasn't an easy decision for me to make.

I would be the star of the show—I liked the sounds of that. I wanted to be a part of this divine play, but I knew that the reality of it all would be far different from the planning of it. Aside from my own difficulties, I could also see the toll this would take on my parents and relatives—the emotional cost was high. We would all do the best we could, but I often questioned myself on whether this was an overly ambitious undertaking on my part.

Why was I willing to take this chance knowing full well what my life was going to be like?

The simple reason was to wake up my loved ones from their sleepy state, so they could grow and expand in ways they may not have otherwise done. Because they are so tough it would take devastation and tragedy to shake them to the core and to push them in the direction they needed to go. Not just one of them, all of them. Something that would affect each one of them individually and force them in the direction of growth that they each required to become the people they are meant to be–including me.

Ribbon of Grace
This is the child God brought to us,
His needs are great of fragileness.
He comes to us of bright light,
To help us claim our God-given rights.
A special child indeed he is,
A shining star amidst the night.
He chose our family to settle in,
His trust was great and from within.
His star bright eyes open wide with love,
Never wavered from the job to be done.
He chose our family not randomly,
But said, "it's there with them, I want to be."
The play was his from the start,
Bringing on stage his family's heart.
Their hearts were bound and wrapped round his,
With the ribbon of Grace from source within.
This beautiful child we gladly take,
To love and care for is no mistake!

Entry 38: 2010

Sitting in Silence

Those first seven years were the most difficult years of my entire life. I never knew anyone could endure so much pain for so long and survive. The trauma of having a swollen brain, seizures, contractures, tubes stuck up my nose and down my throat within seconds of each other, surgeries, feeding tubes, cortical blindness, auditory deficiencies, and severely spastic limbs made it pretty much impossible for me to have any kind of life, let alone enjoy that life in any way.

No one can ever truly know the pain that another person is experiencing. Even if they are in similar circumstances themselves, it is never the same. One can only peer through the looking glass and say, "I understand the pain you're in." But, understanding is NOT the same as *feeling.*

I constantly had to go inward, back to the decision I had made and why I made it. Although it wasn't easy for me, I went deeper inside myself to approach my existence from a different place. Experiencing your suffering from a different place–a different vantage point–pulls you in deep, if you are willing to go. If not, the physical pain will not only brutalize the body, it will also ravage the mind and spirit.

Whether you are aware of it or not, going deep takes you to the heart of it; to the truth of who you are. I suffered extraordinary pain. This was a pain so intense that it made me sit in the silence of spirit and view myself and the world around me from a different perspective than perhaps other people do. If I had not sat in silence, I would have been lost forever in the great pain I experienced. I reminded myself that this agony was for my higher good. But would my purpose here on Earth be served? I didn't know. If I would not have been able to go underneath all the pain and suffering I may have given up the fight to live altogether.

Brave One
Where are you tonight, brave one?
Are you sitting amidst the stars,
Watching them streak by?
Are you twinkling just as they,
Looking down through a haze?

Entry 39: 2009

Surrendering

I never minded being cared for around the clock or that I was dependent on others to take care of my every need. From the very beginning of my life, people took care of me, so I didn't know any other way of living.

As for some individuals, I imagine that it would be very difficult to allow someone to take care of them; it might be especially challenging if they had led an independent life at one time. Perhaps it might feel as though they were less of a person or unworthy in some way to give in and be dependent on someone else.

A fear may seep in. Fear may come from pride or ego and letting go of that fear might be a difficult and painful act for some. Letting go would require relinquishing control of their lives in some way, or maybe they wouldn't want to put someone out if they had once been the strong caregiver.

Most certainly it would be others that needed cared for, and they couldn't fathom the fact that it was themselves that needed help this time. Even in the midst of their confused emotions, regardless of what their fears were, in time they would slowly and gracefully let go and be able to receive the help and care they required from others. They would also grow from the experience in ways they could not have imagined—just as my family did from years of loving and caring for me.

As I am writing this, I realize that I may have had a subconscious problem myself with the nursing care I received; otherwise, why would I have preferred to call my nurses 'valets' under the guise of being too old to call them nurses? As I see things now, the truth of the matter is that I had around the clock nurses—not valets. These were educated RNs and LPNs who loved me, cared for me, and kept me comfortable and healthy to the best of their abilities; they deserve to be called nurses.

If I can have a sudden shift in my perception and heal an issue—while not in the physical form—it would mean that anyone could experience a perceptual shift and a healing, whether they are dead or alive.

Entry 40: 2006

Dreamwalker

In the early years, I was very fragile health-wise. There were times before my miracle when I would become deeply discouraged and think that things would never change. I felt powerless because nothing was in my control; everything was in the hands of my mother and others to do for me. I was tired of fighting for my life by the minute and by the day, but Mom kept going, hoping and knowing that her search would pay off someday.

★★★

When these times of despair came upon me, I would dream. Sometimes these dreams would help me to see myself in a different way. My dreams always came at the right time and when I needed them the most; they gave me hope and kept me going a little while longer.

One night, I dreamt of an old man who was crippled-up in the legs and feet. He was alone; there was only him. With great pain and difficulty, this handicapped man very slowly and heroically made his way up several flights of stairs that were as crooked and funny looking as he was.

At the top of these steps was the doctor that he was going to visit. Each step he took was laborious, long, and excruciatingly painful for him, but he was determined to make it all the way up to the doctor's office. It was clear that he was unwavering in his climb. The elderly gentleman continued to move and partially drag himself up each twisted step.

This old, disabled man never gave up; he didn't quit or say, *"I'm done with this!"* He didn't complain or whine—not even silently to himself. His concentrated focus was on his mission. He was *in* each moment and *in* each step that he took; in that moment—he just was. As I watched this man struggle in his efforts to reach the top step, admiration, love, and compassion for him overcame me.

When I woke up, I remembered the dream and all the emotions I felt towards this crooked old man and his quest. It came to me that the elderly crippled man was like me. I could see the accomplishment and determination of his struggle; he had made progress despite his disability and pain. I realized that the admiration and compassion that I felt toward him in the dream was how I was supposed to see myself. And, no matter how miniscule or small the progress I made seemed, it was a great accomplishment for me.

The moment I understood that the strength it took for me to keep moving forward was amazing, and that I was amazing, the same feelings of wonderment swept through my body. I felt the same admiration, love, and compassion for myself in the same way that I had felt them for the crippled-up man.

I had never looked at myself that way before. I also realized that my mind needed to catch up with my body's progression in health; my mind was used to seeing itself and my body in same old way without shifting its perception as my health improved. This new internal insight showed me that there is always room for growth and expansion, even in the most horrendous of situations.

Entry 41: 2011

Whispering in Gum Gum's Ear

When my grandmother came back from Mexico in the early summer, she told my mom that she was going to California to take a Reconnective Healing® workshop that was offering levels I, II, & III. Grandma had read the book and did all the research on it; she explained to Mom that she felt it might help to practice this healing technique on me. Mom agreed to attend the workshop with Gum Gum, so on the appointed dates, off they went to study Reconnective Healing®.

★★★

My grandmother wasn't sure that taking the level III workshop was necessary and had put off signing up for it. During a break, Grandma went outside and sat by herself. She was almost finished with the second level at this point and needed to quickly make up her mind so she could sign up for level III if she was going to take it.

While Gum Gum was quietly sitting alone, I could see that she needed my help in this decision. She wasn't making any choice at all–she was just sitting there waiting for the answer to come. I knew that when she is undecided about something and can't make up her mind, she won't do anything–she likes to be sure of what she is doing.

At this point, I stepped in and gave Gum Gum the nudge she needed to sign up for the level III class. Grandma knew immediately that it was me who told her to sign up; she was so happy I had helped her that she went and registered right away.

Shortly after that, Grandma saw my mother and told her that I had said to take the third workshop. Next thing I know, my mom was running in to register for the last level too. Both Mom and Grandma always trusted me in the ways I would guide them.

★★★

Mom and Grandma practiced Reconnective Healing® on me many times after they returned from California. I am so glad that I stepped in and gave Grandma the push that motivated her to take that final class because it helped me to be more comfortable in so many unseen ways.

★★★

My dark side is coming out now, because I'm just beginning to realize the power I can wield over my mom and grandma. My grandmother always said that I was a dark horse because my sense of humor was dark and a little warped. I laughed if someone got hurt, *but not seriously hurt*, or I'd snicker if my little brother and sister were yelling and making a racket. I laughed if people were in an argument, and then I chuckled at the absurdity of their argument. No one ever knew what to expect from me or what I would be laughing at next–I kept them all on their toes.

Entry 42: 2007

The Prized Potato Chip

I had another one of my dreams last night, Gum Gum. As usual, it came at the right time and when I needed it the most. I dreamt that I was in the hospital, paralyzed, and propped up in a sitting position. While sitting there, I was thinking about the progress I was not making, when I saw a potato chip bag lying on my bed in front of me. I looked at that chip bag for a few minutes, and then the thought came to me to try to move my arm and get a chip. I had nothing to lose by trying, so I will give this a shot. Who knows… I might even get a potato chip out of it.

With extreme mental focus on my arm, I willed it to come up and move forward. However, my arm was not listening to me very well; it felt heavy and awkward from not being used for so long—the muscles had atrophied.

Ever so slowly, I kept at it. I willed my arm to cooperate with me, so I could have the prized potato chip. I was happy and elated that I was lifting my arm up—no matter how awkward it felt.

I was almost to the prize when I realized I needed to be able to get into the bag and pick the chip up. Okay, at minimum, I need two fingers to work together to get that chip. I tried to move my fingers one at a time; I didn't care which fingers moved, as long as I could move two of them. It happened! I could move two fingers a tiny bit—that would be enough. I only need to move those fingers enough to get that chip.

Now, I am ready to make my move. I feel like a magician sneaking my fingers into that potato chip bag. I feel it, the sought-after chip—the prize. My hand is unsteady, but it is time to move the fingers and do the trick of a magician.

The tips of my fingers caress a chip, and very delicately, I close in on it. There it is. *Carefully...carefully...*close the tips of the fingers on the potato chip. Done. Okay, I have the chip, now what?

Again, I mentally think and will my arm and fingers through the movements—I am not about to lose that chip now. My hand is almost to my mouth; this is going to be tricky hitting the target. My aim is faulty to say the least, and my hand keeps bumping into the side of my mouth. I'm careful, though, because I sure didn't want to break that chip before I got the chance to eat it. I hit the jackpot—the chip goes in my mouth.

I have never tasted anything so good in my life as when

that potato chip went in my mouth. I was beside myself with exuberant excitement and happiness over what I had just done. I had moved my paralyzed arm and two fingers, picked up a potato chip, and ate it.

I felt like I had done a next to impossible thing. The sense of achievement I felt was overwhelming and I was ecstatic about making this kind of progress. I couldn't wait to show my family and friends what I could do. I wasn't going to tell them what I was going to do; I was going to surprise them all.

My family and a few friends came for a visit that evening. I slowly went through all the same concentrated movements that I had done the first time. I wasn't as clumsy and shaky this time and I was a little better at hitting my mouth this time too. This was the second-best chip I had ever had.

I waited expectedly for a response…I waited for someone to recognize the feat I had just performed. To me, this had been a milestone in my recovery and worth mentioning, but no one said anything. It was as if I had done nothing–how could they miss it? I was disappointed and saddened by this.

After my family and friends were done visiting, I just sat there disturbed that no one noticed or commented on what I had done. I had wanted to share the progress I made with them, and I had thought that they would be excited and happy with me. I mean…I was paralyzed all over, but now I could move my arm and two of my fingers–that is progress! Right?

★★★

Then, I woke up feeling kind of sad. I needed some time to process all of this, so I lay in bed quietly hoping to have a better understanding of all that happened in the dream and what this was all about. After some time, it came to me that in my dream I had been proud of myself for the achievement and my progress I had made. No matter how slow and arduous, or what the obstacles, the progress was one of inner growth. No one else could appreciate or see this growth, and it didn't matter.

I was the one that needed to see the growth, be excited about it, be joyful, and to share—in my own special way—my joy and happiness with others. After I realized what the dream meant to me, I suddenly felt as though I had a warm secret inside of me to hold close and I felt good about myself. Once again, I was lifted up by a heaven-sent message in a dream.

Although, I many times thought that direct insight would be a lot easier to understand than a symbolic dream that I had to ponder over. I guess it did help me reach inside of myself and go a little deeper to have a better understanding of myself.

Entry 43: 2006

Heartbridge

I'm in the hospital now; I'm in a real bad way. There's a tube stuck down my throat and taped to my face. My whole body aches and is in so much pain that it is crying. I don't know what's wrong, I just know by the way I'm feeling that this could be it for me. I'm so scared, I feel like I'm going to die. I don't know if I can do this anymore–I'm getting close to letting go. This is too much for me to cope with alone.

Gum Gum is in Mexico. She doesn't know that I'm deathly sick and in the hospital in big trouble. I must get in touch with Gum Gum; she can help–I know it! I need to send her a message...one of my signals on fire (that's how we communicate through spirit) before it's too late. Thank God that Gum Gum can hear and see me when others can't. She'll know what to do!

Grandma sees the signal I sent to her–we create a heart-bridge and she sees me now; she knows that I am in deep trouble. Gum Gum is so strong; she takes me into her arms, comforts me, and talks to me. She is holding onto me so tightly, and she is giving me strength. She is determined not to let me drift away from her.

Now that Gum Gum knows I'm in trouble, and in the hospital, she calls Mom every day to check in on me. I don't know how long my grandma has been holding on to me, but it seems like many days have passed by. The ICU doctors say I'm well enough to be moved to a room, but my mom knows that I won't receive the care I need, so she checks me out of the hospital.

I made it to Gum Gum in time. I made it through this crisis with the help of her healing heart. I can now let go of Grandma and go home with my mom and dad.

Entry 44: 2006

Let's Go to Mexico!

I'm back home now. That trip to the hospital has taken a lot of out of me, and I'm still feeling traumatized and exhausted. It's good to be home, but things here have become extremely stressful. I am supposed to be recovering, but it is very difficult to heal because the stress that's all around me is so intense and prevents me from healing. The nurses are intervening between my mother and the doctors without her knowledge. Mom can't understand who is changing my medication and feeding orders, or why. The nurses are questioning everything Mom does, as if Mom doesn't know how to care for me properly. I guess the nurses are scared for me after what I have been through and are overreacting in a way that is stressful to Mom and me.

My mom sorts out the mess while Gum Gum comes home from Mexico. I'm so glad to see Grandma because she has a solution for getting me out from under the stress, so I can get better. Gummy's idea is to take me to Mexico for a month, so I can recuperate on the beach. She tells Mom that the salt air, ocean, sun, and rest are what I need most right now to recover. She knows I need to get away from everything and everyone that is stressing me out.

Even though she would like to do it, Mom doesn't think it can be done–there is so much involved and to be considered. I hear Gum Gum saying to Mom, "yes, we can do this. I'll help you. We can do this together, Gina."

Gum Gum keeps reassuring my mom that they can take me to Mexico, and that this is what I need to get better. Oh, how I want to do this! If I know my mom... she'll come around after she and grandma figure out a plan.

Entry 45: 2006

Preparations for Mexico

Taking a sick boy like me to Mexico had many considerations to take into account. Gum Gum and Mom listed all the concerns and discussed them. Grandma felt that I should have at least a month there, and Mom agreed with that.

I needed around the clock nursing care. In order to eliminate the stress around me, it was decided that only one nurse would come with us. Mom and Gum Gum chose the nurse who had been with me for many years; she knew me and my ways. She was also a compatible companion for our small group. Gum Gum and Mom would take turns caring for me in the daytime. I really was excited about going, but I was feeling so miserable that it was hard to show my excitement.

My mom ordered a month's supply of what we needed to take:

- My special canned milk
- My medications

- Syringes to administer my medicines
- Catheters for my suction pump
- Saline solution for my nose
- Things for the G-tube port and balloon inside my belly (it is a complicated affair when it comes to things inside my stomach and what can go wrong)
- Chargers and adapters for my equipment
- Diapers

I was still weak, so there could be times when I would need oxygen. With the help of a friend, my grandma arranged for oxygen tanks to be on hand when I arrived at our house in Mexico.

Planning for the airplane ride was also crucial. My health was very fragile, and traveling would be the most difficult thing for me to do without an incident. Gum Gum and Mom were very aware of this, but they were on a mission to give me a better chance of healing, the time I would need to heal, and a place that was better suited for it.

Entry 46: 2006

Days of Wonderment and Bliss

I flew to Mexico without a glitch; it was a well-laid plan. We picked up my oxygen tanks and Gum Gum drove my gang and me to our house. My first day there, Mom took me over to Gum Gum's house, which was next door. Gum Gum put a lounge chair on the terrace that overlooked the Gulf of Mexico and the swimming pool. Next, she put blankets, towels, and pillows on the lounge chair to make it more comfortable for me—her boy—to lie on.

It was time for me to be taken out of my wheelchair and lounge around like a lazy lad. I was good and ready to lay around after that long trip to Mexico. I was made comfortable and as I sprawled out on this beautiful, spectacular day, with an amazing view of the ocean, I felt like I came down ten notches. *Does that make sense to you? I hope it does!*

Gum Gum stayed with me, and Mom went back to our house. The longer I laid there, the more I felt like I had died and gone to heaven. It was so peaceful and quiet—just me, Gum Gum, and ocean waves. There were no nurses coming and going, no stress. I was on my way to healing already and was looking forward to a month of lying around; and that is exactly what I did for one whole month. I laid on Gum Gum's terrace every day, soaking up the salt air and listening to the waves. I felt so blissful and happy; it is so amazing to feel this way. This was something I never experienced before, I didn't even know it was possible to feel like this. I started feeling better, so Gum Gum and Mom put me in the swimming pool for brief periods of time. It was a month of wonderment and healing for me.

All the feelings and thoughts of, *I have had enough...I think I am ready to go home now...I can't do this any longer... my spirit being is so tired and weary of it all,* were lifted from me. Now I knew I would live and that I would stay here with my family a while longer–this was the turning point for me. Grandma knew when I decided to stay with them and told everyone I was okay, that everything would be all right.

★★★

This trip to Mexico was the best thing that could have been done for me at that time. Gum Gum and Mom had the courage, determination, and tenacity to take me to Mexico in spite of what everyone else thought about it. Mom and Gum Gum knew me better than anyone else, and they knew what was best for me.

Waves of Transformation
The ocean swells up,
Moves through the waves
Transforming the slightest debris.
Now calm and in tune,
Waves move in harmony
With the unseen.

Entry 47: 2007

All Hail King Brady

When we went to Mexico on vacation, we used to visit the Mayan ruins at Edzna. We would also always make it a point to visit an old sugar plantation, Hacienda Uayamon, which is situated in the middle of the jungle about a half hour from Edzna. We would make a whole day of it; this was our own special tradition, you might say.

Our routine was to go to Edzna first; it was a quiet, beautiful place with an air of other worldliness from a time long past that seemed to pull you in. I often felt like I was suspended in time while there. Big iguanas were roaming and climbing around everywhere, and birds were chirping and flying around. There was a quietude at Edzna that felt good to me.

We would then go to Hacienda Uayamon for lunch, which I loved. Afterward, we swam in the beautiful pools that were on the hotel grounds.

★★★

The first time we went to Hacienda Uayamon, as we got to the bottom of the stairs that led up to the restaurant, everyone stopped and looked up. There were several flights of stone steps leading to the restaurant, and it was a very high, steep climb. Everyone kept staring at the stairs. Gum Gum asked, "oh God, how do we get Brady all the way up there?" My family just continued standing there, thinking about the predicament we were in. Suddenly, from out of nowhere, four waiters appeared. The servers—all four of them—picked me up in my wheelchair and carried me up all those steps. Everyone agreed that I looked like royalty, like a king, being hand-carried up those stairs. I felt like a king too! A laughing king, at that!

Riding in the Back of a Pickup

We had always talked about going to see a nighttime laser light show at Edzna. Although we had been to the ruins many times, inevitably we were never there at the right time for the laser show. This time was the right time though.

A plan was put into place and the whole family (Mom, Dad, Grandma, Charlie, Riley, a nurse, and one of our friends) drove to Edzna. It was a treacherous, dark road to drive and it took over an hour and a half to get there in the backcountry of Mexico. None of us knew what to expect, we had never been to a laser show before. The closer we got, the more excited everyone was. It was a dark and mysterious night, which only added to the excitement.

We finally arrived. The question of how I was going to get back to the ruins in the dark, and over the stones and rough ground, was the problem. As my parents were discussing this, a man in a pickup truck drove up to us. Our friend explained our dilemma to the truck driver and asked if I could be put in the back end of his pickup truck.

★★★

Sitting in the bed of this rough pickup seemed a little shaky to me—just imagine me precariously perched high up there in my wheelchair. I wasn't too sure that this was safe.

After figuring out how to secure me and my wheel-chair in the back of the truck, it was decided that this was how I was going to get to the site of the laser show. I stiffened up and readied myself for the four men that were coming at me. They easily lifted me up into the bed of the truck and I was positioned, then each man took hold of my wheelchair to keep me from rolling out of the tailgate. I was riding high, as I was perched up there like a bird on a swing; I rocked and rolled and swayed back and forth like a bird too.

While I was being driven in my own special coach, my family walked back to the ruins. They arrived just in time to see me coming across the large open field in front of the pyramids, sitting grandly in the back end of an old, and *I mean very old,* rusty pickup. My family laughed at the spectacle of me riding high like a Mayan king in front of all the people who were waiting to see the show. I braced myself again as the four men lifted me down off the tailgate and very gently handed me, their charge, over to my parents.

The laser show on the ruins was fantastic! Everyone oohed and aahed as the colors changed and shifted in form. Being out in the night, with the stars overhead, only enhanced the show more.

When the spectacle was over, the pickup truck returned, and I was again hoisted up into the back end of it. Only this time, I did not stiffen up and get big-eyed with the thought of riding in the back of the truck. I knew that the bumpy ride would be fun, and I'd laugh all the way back to the van where my family was waiting for me.

Entry 49: 2009

Glorious Mexican Sunshine

Champotòn is a little Mexican town located about twenty-five minutes from our house and is the closest place to buy food and supplies. One morning, my mother went grocery shopping in Champotòn, so I was left at home in the care of two valets. My grandmother was next door at her house.

One of my valets decided that I could use some beautiful Mexican sunshine, so she wheeled me outside onto the terrace and parked me in the shade. It truly was glorious, soaking up the sunshine and listening to the ocean waves. It was glorious for about forty-five minutes!

I became more and more uncomfortable. The valets didn't seem to notice what was happening to me, and they probably thought I was having a grand old time enjoying this glorious Mexican sunshine. I was sitting in the shade, so I must have appeared fine to them.

After about two hours (this is my best guess because I can't tell time), my grandmother came over to check on me. She took one look at my face and knew that no one had put sunscreen on me; I was bright red all over and all puffed up–I looked and felt like a lobster. Gum Gum immediately pushed me inside and asked the valets why they left me outside so long without applying sunscreen to my skin. The valets told her that they had put sunscreen on me, but I'm sure my grandma didn't believe them. Gum Gum applied a lotion to my sunburn and tried to ease the pain I was in. She could be a tiger where me and my care was concerned, and she never hesitated to step in to help me if she felt it was necessary to do so.

My mother returned home, only to find me severely sunburnt, blistered, and crying. I was so sick from the sunburn that I had a fever and I needed oxygen to sleep at night. Aloe vera gel and cold washcloths were put on my skin. The only thing that calmed me was my mother or brother pushing me around the house in my wheelchair (they did this for hours on end to make me feel better).

Mom questioned the valets, but there were no good answers and they would not assume any responsibility for actions they had or had not taken. It took some time and pain for me to recover from the first sunburn I ever had, but eventually I healed, and I can say that I never wanted to experience another sunburn again.

Entry 50: 2009

Marketplace

Today is the day we are going to Champotòn, the little town closest to us. We are all loaded up now, and I'm in my seat with all my contraptions to keep me sitting upright. I am really looking forward to this day trip because we are going to the open marketplace. I haven't been to the market yet, but Gum Gum has. I don't know what to expect at this bazaar.

★★★

Well, the trip was full of surprises that I had not antici-
pated. One such surprise was that not everyone went to
the market. My grandmother parked the van in town and
her and my mom got my wheelchair out and situated me
in it. Unexpectedly, Mom announced that she was going
to the grocery store while Gum Gum, Charlie, Riley and
I were going to the open market.

Gum Gum and us kids started the trek across the street
to the market. Grandma pushed my wheelchair, while
Charlie and Riley walked on either side. The outside
temperature was quite warm, and the smells of cooking
food in the open market floated through the air to greet
us the closer we got.

Once inside the bazaar, we just stood there looking
around the strange place. Charlie, Riley, and I had never
seen anything like this during our whole lives; it was
packed with old, wooden stalls that were sky high and
overflowing with goods. I saw raw, dead chickens, pigs,
hunks of beef, and all kinds of different animals hanging
from large hooks that were attached to the top of the stalls.

If it wasn't meats of some sort hanging down, it was
vegetables, dresses, shirts, and all sorts of clothing hanging
up or draped across the stalls. Fruits, vegetables, candies,
or any food of your liking were there in the market, there
was even jewelry—it was one big wooden maze of stuff to
buy! It was a lot for me to take in.

On one end of the maze, there was a fish market. Fish,

pulpa (my new favorite Spanish word), crab, and lobster were being sold everywhere. Here you could choose the kind, size, and quantity of seafood you desired; if you wanted it filleted, a fisherman would fillet it right there in front of you.

The marketplace was busy with people shopping, eating, and talking. Shoppers haggled with stall owners over the cost of what they wanted to buy and what they wanted to pay for the item. Gum Gum pushed me around so I could see and smell everything.

The day grew hotter and hotter the longer we were there. Everyone knows that you don't go into town midday because the heat can become unbearable. Here we were, midday...and Mom still hadn't come back yet.

I was sweating profusely, and so were Charlie and Riley—we all had red faces. Gum Gum looked like she was ready to drop at any minute. Her hair, shirt, and face were dripping wet, and it looked like she had been swimming in a hot tub. I was thinking, *oh please, God, don't let anything happen to my Gum Gum...she is all we have here in this strange, foreign place.* Mom is here now to rescue us; she looks ready to be done with it now too.

★★★

We never did buy anything at the open marketplace, but I will say that it was quite an experience on all accounts. I don't want to do that again any time too soon though.

Entry 51: 2011

I Love to Swim

When I was in Mexico, Grandma and Mom would help me into Grandma's swimming pool. It wasn't the easiest thing either, getting me into the pool. There weren't any steps and I was deadweight, unable to help in any way. Gum Gum and I were always a little nervous and scared about putting me in the pool, not to mention my concern that I might be dropped. This was a precarious maneuver, and I tried to always keep a calm look on my face so as not to show my alarm and make matters worse. Mom and Grandma lowered me into the swimming pool with as much care as possible.

Sometimes my mom and grandma would take me into the ocean; now that was interesting to watch. As I grew, it proved to be difficult getting me down the beach and into the water; this was a problem. My dad had the thought to buy a plastic orange toboggan; in his mind, this was the answer—to pull me through the sand to the water's edge.

The orange toboggan was lined with towels so my head wouldn't bounce and roll around the sled and get hurt. Mom and Grandma carefully laid me down in the sled and pulled it through the sand, then gently guided it into the water. Once in the ocean, it was easy to pick me up and put me in the water. I had a life jacket on, which was helpful. Someone would have to hold my head out of the water, otherwise, it would just drop down into the ocean and I could swallow saltwater.

Whether I was in the pool or the ocean I felt free and weightless. I would kick my legs and feel the movement making waves that splashed me in the face, or I would sometimes feel a little nibble on my foot or leg from a fish and I would laugh. Sometimes, I would just float. My body was not restrained like it was in a wheelchair; this is what I loved the most.

Waterfall

The waterfall splashes down on me,
My face upturned toward the sky.
I inhale the water and the trees,
And all there is for me.

Entry 52: 2011

Fish Out of Water

The day started out bright and sunny. Mom got me ready for an adventure at the beach by putting swimming eye goggles, earplugs, and sunscreen on my body. Once I was ready, Dad laid me down in his makeshift plastic toboggan raft and pulled me across the beach down to the water's edge.

I was lying in my toboggan raft as I floated in the ocean. I was enjoying this floaty feeling, it was as though someone were rocking me gently in my own special little boat. Now and again, a small wave would splash up and sprinkle me with water drops. I didn't mind so much because it was a hot day, and the ocean felt refreshing and cooled me down.

I was minding my own business when suddenly something changed, and I noticed that the waves were getting rougher. I was being bounced around more and more. Dad was hanging on to me, so I wasn't too worried–I knew he wouldn't let anything happen to me. WRONG! The wind picked up, the waves started rolling over me, and saltwater rushed into my mouth. Now I was getting concerned, and I was ready to go into shore. I tried to make faces and noises to inform Dad that I wasn't happy, but he wasn't catching on to my gestures very quickly.

After realizing that I was getting hit by waves, my dad finally started pulling me into shore. I grew increasingly impatient with him because he was going at the pace of a snail. We almost made it, but just as we were reaching shore the biggest wave ever hit me full on. It covered me with saltwater and sand and rocked me around the toboggan raft like a piece of driftwood. I started kicking and screaming. Dad decided to speed it up and move faster; he hurriedly worked at getting me pulled onto the sand by the edge of the water. All the while, even more saltwater full of sand hit me, tossing me around again and again. It was too late...I was good and mad now! I had never been this angry before. Sandy saltwater was up my nose and in my ears; it had even gotten up under my goggles and into my eyes. Now my eyes were burning from saltwater, sand, and tears. I even lost my custom-made earplugs.

Gum Gum came running down to the shore when she heard the commotion. I saw Grandma looking down at me with a distressed look of concern on her face when she saw the condition I was in. What she saw was me with my goggles askew and my body covered in saltwater and sand, writhing around in the toboggan. But wait...I also saw a glimpse of something else behind her eyes. I know what Gum Gum wanted to do–she wanted to laugh. I couldn't believe this! I was in a disastrous state and still she wanted to laugh at me, so I was mad at her too. Grandma had never seen me this furious before and she wanted to laugh about it–I didn't care, I was still mad at her.

My dad saw how I looked with sandy saltwater all over my body and quickly drug the sled up the beach towards the house. Not paying attention, my dad pulled the sled's rope higher and higher into the air until the toboggan flipped me over onto the hot sand. This just topped it off for me, it was the final nail in the toboggan. Hot sand stuck to my body everywhere. I was seething inside at my dad. I felt like a dirty, salty, sandy, wet, kicking, screaming, raving mad, floundering fish on the beach! This added insult to injury. My dad kept saying repeatedly, "I'm sorry, I'm sorry, I'm sorry." I didn't care, it would be a while before I got over this disaster of his caretaking.

Considering that sand does not come off easily, it just kind of sticks to your skin, I was washed and showered off as quickly as possible. I felt better once I was toweled off and wearing clean, dry clothes. It took a little while for me to let go of my madness, but eventually I did. I know that even now when my family thinks of that time on the beach, they all laugh at how mad I was. Difference is...I know they laugh with love for me and the bodyguard, my dad.

Entry 53: 2010

Crooked Little Boy

How do I bend my arms, wrists, and legs if they are all crooked and stiff? I don't. I can move them to a certain degree, but someone else has to bend my legs and arms for me.

When I become spastic–from being upset, sick, or from laughing–there is no way of bending my limbs at all; my whole body is straight and stiff as a board. My arms turn and twist almost backwards; my wrists and hands also twist and bend backwards, but in a different direction than my arms.

To have a T-shirt put on me involves a caregiver manually bending my arm at the elbow and bringing my arm towards my chest, then turning my arm just enough to work my hand through the armhole. At the same time, my wrist has to be twisted to bend my elbow. How far my arm can be bent and turned is important to know, to avoid a fracture while dressing me.

The more I grew, the more difficult it became for someone to perform this manipulation of my wrist, elbow, and arm, as my bones slowly kept bending and twisting in whichever way they wanted and would stay in that certain position until slowly they moved again into an even worse position.

Sometimes when Gum Gum would put my shirt on me, she had to stop and start all over again if she knew she wasn't getting it quite right. She always got it on, but on occasion, she would get a little frustrated in the process because she didn't want to hurt me. She was careful and methodical in this procedure of putting on my T-shirts.

The physical therapist had a secret trick for bending my arms—she firmly pushed down on the top of my hand at the wrist. This little maneuver opened my hand and allowed my arm to be bent much easier at the elbow (Mom used this trick on my younger siblings too).

My hands had to be opened finger by finger, from a fist position, in order to wash my hands or put the splints on that were supposed to help keep them open. Every part of my arm, from my shoulder down to my fingers, had to be turned, twisted, and bent ever so slowly, in just the right way, to have a T-shirt put on me.

Now, my legs I consider to be not as badly bent and twisted; not like the rest of my body from the hips up. Having my pants put on me wasn't nearly as difficult as having shirts put on. I wore mostly stretchy waistbands for ease and comfort.

My feet and toes were always so swollen that it was difficult to find shoes that would accommodate my feet and splints. Socks were easy to put on me, obviously. Gum Gum loved to bring me cool socks from Mexico; one pair had red chili peppers on them and another pair had green iguanas. She liked to make socks interesting for me. Now came the shoes and I would be all set, except for one other thing. I wanted to keep this for last to tell you…it's not easy telling the world, or whoever reads this, that before my pants were put on I had to have a diaper put on me.

Entry 54: 2012

A Suitcase Full of Bananas

Something is up, because everyone is bustling around and getting out their suitcases. We must be getting ready for another trip. My nurse is going around my room not only gathering up some of my clothes but picking up some of my toys and packing them too. I know I am going somewhere for sure now. I don't think we are leaving until morning though, because all my equipment is still in its place.

I hear Mom and Grandma talking about Philadelphia and us staying there for two weeks. It must be that Mom and Gum Gum have something new for me to do or try, and I can feel the excitement starting to build inside of me now. I am going to have trouble sleeping tonight for sure. I'll be thinking about where I'm going and all the fun I'll be having.

★★★

This morning, after my nurse showered and dressed me,

my suction pump, oxygen tank, and special milk were all packed up. Mom and Gum Gum brought a lot of suitcases into my room. There's a ramp outside my entrance door that makes it practically effortless to get my wheelchair out of the house, and as an added bonus, it's also much easier to take suitcases out my door too.

I think Charlie packed her own bag this time because Mom asked her if she brought everything she needed. Charlie tells Mom that yes, she did. Riley says that he did too; I almost started to laugh when my mom asked them if they were packed. I can picture it now…Riley would have a suitcase full of bananas, crackers, candy, apples, grapes, and maybe, just maybe, a T-shirt–these are his go-to reserves.

Riley packed his bag once when he was about four years old and was going to go away on a trip with Grandma. Riley was so excited to be traveling with Gum Gum that he packed his bag long before he was actually leaving. About two weeks later, Dad saw Riley's little suitcase and opened it up to see what was inside. What my dad found was a supply of smelly bananas, rotten apples, and a bag of chipped ham all decayed and black; there were fruit flies everywhere in the suitcase. I guess he wanted to get a head start in making sure he was ready to go.

A suitcase full of baby dolls would be Charlie's thing. I can't wait to see what they have packed…it's going to be amusing and will give me a good laugh.

Entry 55: 2012

Trapeze Artist

I'm still not sure what this trip is all about, but I do know it has to do with me and I know that we are in Philadelphia. This morning we are all loaded into my van and Gum Gum is driving, as usual. The place we are going is called a myofascial release therapy clinic. I'm not sure what that means, but I'm looking forward to finding out.

The clinic is a very nice place; everyone is friendly and welcoming. A therapist is coming out to get me, it's my turn! The therapist, Mom, and Grandma come with me into a room. Mom undresses me, except for my diaper, and lays me down on a massage table; I feel a little chilly without my clothes on. Pictures and measurements of my whole body are taken at every angle. The therapist does reflex testing on me too, and everything is written down. Boy, they are interested in me! I like this already.

This is different from when I usually go to see regular doctors; there is a gentle, caring feel to how these people handle me. These therapists understand that the way they choose to move my body can be painful for me, and they do their best not to hurt me as they move my arms, legs, feet, hands, and head around.

Every day for two weeks I am taken to the myofascial clinic for therapy. There are two to five therapists working on me at a time. Sometimes Gum Gum and Mom are asked to help the therapists support me; the head guy shows them what to do.

I am going to try to explain, the best I can, how this kind of therapy works. It's rather hard though, because I was so relaxed and haven't been paying as close attention to what they are doing as I should. The therapists pressed on certain muscles with their hands until they felt pressure. When the muscle softened, more pressure was applied until it softened again; this was done many times until each layer of muscle was soft and relaxed. The purpose in doing this was to release any emotional traumas trapped in the muscle and fascia tissue. My body "unwinds" in different ways after the muscle is relaxed and I am even more deeply at ease.

★★★

Gum Gum says that when the muscle softens under her fingers it feels like her fingers are moving through creamy butter.

★★★

During my first myofascial release treatment, I was "unwinding" up in the air, as five therapists, Gum Gum, and Mom were holding my body up and allowing it to unfold. It seemed to twist and turn in whatever ways it wanted to, needed to, in order to release the trauma that it had been holding onto for so long. To Mom, it looked like I was being birthed in midair.

I was twisting and turning like a high-wire act at the circus, the experience was awesome! Not only did I feel like I was floating, but I also felt like I had released something big. I felt fluid and dreamy. I slept and rested well in this dreamy state too, much better than I ever had before coming to the clinic. Something had changed for me, but it's one of those things you can't quite put your finger on. You know you're different somehow, in a good way, but it's difficult to describe.

★★★

It was time to go home now; my two weeks at the clinic were over. I felt like I had let go of a lot of things in those two weeks. I'm not even sure what I let go of, but it doesn't matter; I knew I had by how I felt.

Entry 56: 2012

Shopping Spree

I continued to go and see the neurologist in Florida for some years. Throughout this period, the doctor continued to add new protocols to help me improve even more. I progressed slowly, and eventually learned to answer questions by blinking "yes" or "no."

My mom taught me how to communicate this way by asking me test questions and saying, "now Brady, blink two times for 'yes,' and one time for 'no.'" I slowly got better at blinking answers and would have a quicker response for Mom.

My grandmother was away on a trip when I learned

how to communicate by blinking, I was excited for her to come back and see what I could do now. When Grandma came back, Mom said to her, "guess what Brady can do?" Well, Grandma had no idea how to answer that question. Mom told her, "Brady can blink 'yes' or 'no' if you ask him a question; two blinks for 'yes,' one blink for 'no.' Let's go ask Brady a question."

Grandma came back to my room with Mom. She said to me, "Brady, your mom says that you can answer questions now." I think she was a little bit skeptical by the way she said that to me, though. She continued, "I'm going to ask you a question very slowly so that you understand." Gum Gum bent down in front of my face (and while she is doing this I am wondering why she is getting in my face like this) and very slowly she asked, "Brady do you like my hair?" I had to mess with her a little bit, so I took my time in giving her a clear one blink "no."

I gave her a minute to think about my answer before I gave her a two blink "yes." She saw my two blinks and started laughing and said, "that's my Brady messing with me again." She was so excited and happy that she and I could communicate in another way now.

★★★

We were shopping at the biggest mall in the world for souvenir T-shirts and back to school clothes. My brother and sister chose matching superhero T-shirts. Charlie and Riley wanted me to buy the same one, so our mom asked me if I wanted the same superhero shirt as the one they chose. I made myself clear and gave Mom a long, slow, one blink "NO." There was no way I was going to wear that baby shirt. Everyone laughed, realizing as I did, that the T-shirt was definitely too young and goofy for me.

Mom and Gum Gum went around the department store and brought back half a dozen shirts for me to choose from; they held them up in front of me one at a time to see if any of them received my approval, which they did not. So off Mom and Gum Gum went again in search of more T-shirts that were up to snuff.

Finally, there was a two-blink shirt! A guy souvenir shirt, a shirt with a touch of dark humor to it that showed everyone just how I roll. Everyone was relieved and happy that I had finally found the T-shirt I wanted.

Entry 57: 2012

Sedona Workshop

Gum Gum and Mom are leaving for Sedona, Arizona today for a weeklong myofascial release therapy workshop. My myofascial release therapy intensive at the clinic in Philadelphia was such a success that Gum Gum and Mom decided to learn this therapy themselves. They wanted to learn how to practice myofascial release so that either one of them could give me this kind of treatment to help me feel better and be more relaxed. They eventually became very good at it, especially when it came to working on me, I must say.

Entry 58: 2012

The Spark Inside Us All

I was in a contemplative mood this day, as I lay in bed. Suddenly, I saw and felt how I had come into this life-form. I was a divinely joyous spark of excited, exploding light shooting downward like a falling star. I effortlessly slipped into the newborn form waiting for me. I felt a *click* as I slid into the physical form, it was as if I had been locked into place.

These feelings of celestial elation, of when I came here, were so powerful that I thought, *"I wonder what it's like to leave this body."* I had no sooner finished the thought when I felt the most exulted, glorious feeling start to move in waves throughout my body. I felt the edges of my form soften and melt away. My essence slowly lifted and floated upward, out of my body form, in brilliant sparks and sparkles of light particles. I was no longer tethered to or encumbered by my body. A sense of freedom, unlike any I had ever known in this life, took over as I once again became my divine true self.

★★★

I just laid there for the longest time, swept up in this loving, wonderful, unexpected experience and the feelings of it. Something had been lifted and I noticed that there was a change in me. I needed a minute to put my finger on the change…what was different, and gone, at the same time. There it is, I got it! I wasn't afraid to die. My fear of death had been driven away by this single mystical experience.

I felt good, elated at this gift I had been given; I had forgotten how it was when I came here into form on March 23, 1997. Now knowing this, I can recall the exuberant flicker of light that I am and not be scared anymore of how it is going to be when my time is up, because I already know!

Falling Stars

In great excitement,
We fall like stars,
Slipping into form.
Filled with love,
And laughter born.
Entering like a brilliant star,
Clicking into place.
We wonder how
Does it feel,
To leave this space?
A glorious exaltation
Then takes place.
Edges of form melt away!

Entry 59: 2012

Music to Die For

The day I died began several days before. I was slowly losing my life force and I could feel it moving out from my form. I could feel my essence moving throughout my bedroom and even into my grandmother's bedroom.

Although my grandmother could see and feel all these things, she was still unaware or in denial of what was taking place at this time. What she did was play a CD of heavenly healing music. She played it over and over again in the hopes of it giving me strength and comfort, and to help me get through the bad spells I was experiencing.

I believe that heavenly music also gave her comfort as well. I had been having some very bad periods of coughing and turning blue—I felt like I was suffocating. Each time this happened, my nurse, mother, and grandmother would sit me up in bed and clap me on the back and chest until I came back and coughed up the plug of mucus that was lodged in my chest. Then I could breathe again.

Each time though, it was getting harder and harder and it took longer for them to bring me back. My grandmother continued to play the healing music CD. I got lost in the magical sounds of the musical instruments moving through me in such a peaceful and calming way.

Grandma did some energy healing on me; it seemed she was a little discouraged because my energy was so close to my body that she could barely feel it. My mother did myofascial release therapy on my nose and mouth to relax me.

It was time for me to go and I knew it. I was not afraid, though. Now, I'm ready to let my body's physical form soften and melt away.

Rapture
Out I come, from the shell.
Glorious rapture, I take flight.
I am the ocean and the breeze.
I am the stars in the night, sparkling bright.

Entry 60: 2012

November 6th

The day I left this world, I filled my room and my grandmother's room with particles of glorious light that permeated everything and everyone that was there with me. I saw my mother holding me close in her arms and my grandmother standing right next to her, while the nurse was on the other side of the bed. I could feel their kisses and love pouring over me as though I were still alive and in my body.

Gum Gum picked Charlie and Riley up at school and brought them home so they could see me. My dad, who was at work, came as soon as he got word that I had left.

When my dad came in, he sat beside me for a very long time. Although I had already left my body, I was still there, so I covered him with my magnificent sparkles of light and love. I wanted him and everyone else in the room to feel the love and closeness I felt for them in a way that I was never able to express while I was alive.

As I was being wheeled out on the cart, which takes you away to ready you for your final bow on stage, my mother and grandmother followed me outside; they fell into each other's arms sobbing as my lifeless body was loaded into the ambulance. Even though Mom and Grandma knew what they saw was just my empty shell, it represented to them something they could touch and love in the physical, and now they would never be able to do any of that again.

P.S. Remember when I told you my mother and grandmother were tough cookies? Well, I heard my mom make two business calls before calling the coroner–I found this quite amusing.

I Am Enough
When I go home it's with no regrets.
I'm on the mountain of gloriousness.
Sing me a song of beauteousness.
In the starry sky, above I look.
And know I am enough!!

Entry 61: 2012

My Last Act

My last stage act was quite surprising to many people, including my family, because no one realized how many friends I had until they all showed up at the funeral home to see my last act.

I enjoyed another life that few people knew anything about. I had school friends, teachers, and nurses outside of my family life. They all remembered me, loved me, and came to let me know that they cared and to say their goodbyes.

I was lying in my stunningly handsome wooden eternity case with rope carved around it (my mother had it made up special just for me). My Gum Gum looked at me laying in that box and said to Mom, "that's not our Brady, he's not there…he's gone."

Serving God
I came here willing with love full up.
To see the smiles of happiness.
Has been my pleasure,
To serve the God from within.
I am the twinkle of heaven's dust,
Whether here, there, or anywhere.
I see the smiles I came to see
And know you are, still with me.

Entry 62: 2012

Quilt of Many Colors

After my passing, my mom went to Los Angeles, my dad went back to work, and my brother and sister went to school. One day, while my mother was gone, I saw Gum Gum gathering up all my T-shirts. At first, I wasn't sure what the heck she was doing. I soon realized that she was going to make a quilt from all of my shirts.

Gum Gum sorted through my vast collection and chose all of my favorite T-shirts first. She then selected other ones that she thought I may have liked. Gum Gum proceeded to cut large squares from each one of them. The squares were pictures of my favorite things...logos, dolphins, turtles, skulls.

After Gum Gum finished cutting out the squares, she wondered how she could make a quilt; even though she knew how to sew, it had been a long time since she had sewn anything. Gum Gum wanted this quilt to be special and perfect, and she felt that she couldn't do it justice.

So, Gum Gum called a friend of my mother's that knew how to make quilts. Grandma told her what she wanted to do, and that Mom was out of town, so she wanted to finish the T-shirt quilt before she came back. The quilter agreed to help Grandma as a special favor to my Mom.

Gum Gum went to a fabric store to buy more materials for the special quilt. She wanted this gift to be for me and my family, so it had to be special; it had to have unique materials that meant something to me. She chose dolphins, turtles, and all the things that I loved in the materials that she chose to finish the quilt with. I was always in the back of her mind in every choice that she made, to the point of agonizing over her choices, which was silly in a way because I loved all of what she was doing and would have loved anything that she chose.

★★★

Speaking of T-shirts…
There was one T-shirt in particular that I loved to wear because I could tease the nurses with it. It was a bright orange one that read "MAMA SAYS I'M SPECIAL" on the front of the shirt. I think a few of my nurses were offended by it and took it a bit too personal, though. I, on the other hand, found it amusing to wear and see how people reacted to my "MAMA SAYS I'M SPECIAL" T-shirt. Often times, my mother could not find my "offensive" shirt and would search throughout my dresser drawers and my bedroom for it. Eventually my mom would find the T-shirt, and with my humorous dark sense of playfulness intact I would wear my bright orange shirt to school.

Quilted Love
Quilt of colors that are me.
Warmth and comfort come from me.
Love sewn in colors bright,
Come hold me tight,
And rest with me.

Entry 63: 2012

Clueless

The first Christmas after I left, my family went to Mexico; I believe they went there because it was my favorite place to visit. My grandmother was already in Mexico and waiting for their arrival.

The quilter finished the special T-shirt quilt and my grandmother wanted to give it to my parents on Christmas morning. Since Gum Gum was already in Mexico, she didn't know how to get the special quilt there without spoiling the surprise for my parents. Suddenly, an idea came to Grandma…she would have the quilter give the quilt to my great grandmother and then my great grandmother would give it to my mother and tell her that it was a gift to be given to Gum Gum once they arrived in Mexico.

The quilter, my great grandma, and Gum Gum all agreed on this plan of action. So, the quilter dropped it off at my great grandmother's house, who wrapped it in Christmas wrapping paper and took the wrapped gift to my mother. Great Grandma told Mom that the present was for her daughter, my grandma, and asked her to please take it to Mexico for her. My mom carried the wrapped gift all the way to Mexico and gave it to Gum Gum. Mom and Dad didn't have a clue as to what was really going on.

Entry 64: December 25, 2012

Woven with Love

Christmas morning came, and my grandma gave the special Christmas present to my parents. My mom was confused about the whole affair because she still thought the gift was for Gum Gum, but she went ahead and opened it anyway.

After opening the gift, Mom wasn't quite sure what it was that she was looking at. Then, the gift slowly revealed itself to her… it was me, *Brady*, in a quilt. I was woven throughout the quilt in the shape of squares–quilt squares consisting of brilliant colors designed with love by my Gum Gum.

My mom and dad were very quiet for a long time. They really didn't know what to say or how to react to the gift. The quilt served as an in-your-face reminder of the freshness of my passing that saddened them deeply, but at the same time, the quilt was something they could feel me in. Their Brady lived in these squares and colors that he so loved.

My quilt is a part of their lives and it is always draped over a couch or a chair in the living area, and it moves from one person to another. In using the quilt, my love is felt, warmth is felt, and comfort is felt because I am woven throughout every thread of it. *I am the quilt of many colors.*

Sweet Song
I am so grateful that I have been,
The object of so many loves.
If I could whisper in the wind,
All the places I've seen and been,
If I could shout and sing out loud,
It would be, to those I love.
My mouth is quiet and sewn shut,
I hope you hear me,
No matter what.
My song is sweet and fragrant still,
To those I love and always will.

★★★

With this I am finished with the telling of my life, I laid down my golden pen. I knew full well that I may forget all the memories I just wrote down in my dolphin journal. There were so many more recollections that I could have written down, but I knew in my heart that my family remembered me and loved me. I was always there in their thoughts, and sometimes I was even there with them in spirit.

I had been told that when I finished writing my journal it would be put in the Hall of Records for safe keeping. With these thoughts in mind, I picked up my golden pen and slid it into the secret pocket that was hidden inside the journal. As soon as I slid the pen into place, the journal immediately began to glow. I felt ecstatic over this new development.

I could go to the library anytime I wanted and take my

journal down from the shelf to read about my life when I was in physical form. My journal would be easy to find; it would be the glowing book with the name "Brady" on it. If only my parents and family could see it glowing so beautifully!

Brady's Message

These words are peaceful words meant to heal and are coming from a place of love for my family. These words are meant to raise up the lives of my loved ones and those they touch.

It is time for everyone to know the peace that lies beyond this world. The many and the few will rise up in joy for what is to come. I am an emissary of light called to destroy the evils of this world that hold people captive.

My family is one of many called to do this work. Bring light where there is darkness and chaos. These words will reach many in the years to come. I came in the form of a broken boy in order to reach as many as possible in this lifetime.

I personally was not broken but formed from light particles of God Source. I came to weave the light through my family and everyone that knew me, to sit softly and quietly, and watch this light grow and move through everyone so they could spread the light also—even if unknowingly.

The spark that flies and lives in each of us knows no boundaries, for it is pure light, so hold this light in our hearts and watch it grow. See this spark as God's light and share it with others.

This is what will be remembered as a healing time, a time of joy, a time of loving for all mankind. This message is one of love and to stay close to your heart at all times.

The times at hand are revealed as dark times; but, they are not—they are of Love and Light.

BRADY SLOAN PARIS

March 23, 1997 – November 6, 2012

Heart of Gold
Speak softly without words,
Use the gift that rests within.
It stirs the soul with threads of gold,
And shouts louder than words ever did.

PART III

Gum Gum

On the Treadmill

The Fairytale Begins

The Fairytale Ends

On the Treadmill

She was on the treadmill this day. She liked to keep in shape as best she could, considering her years. Time had been good to her in a natural way. She appeared to look and feel younger than her years, so she kept up her daily routine on the treadmill. She was happy; it was only occasionally that she missed the holding of another's hand.

She had four children, two of which were twenty years younger than her first two; they were considered by her to be unexpected miracles because she was told she would never conceive again. She loved all her children with a passion, though, because while they were all so different, they were still similar in many respects. They were the same in the ways that they loved each other and her unconditionally, which is what she adored most about them.

The large bay windows where the treadmill stood allowed her to be wrapped in the embrace of the light coming through. There was snow on the ground and trees that surrounded the house in a quiet solitude. *A good place to write*, she thought. She hadn't considered herself to be a writer until now. Her daughter had recently told her in a firm, strong voice, "Mom, just start writing." As she began she found that she did, in fact, enjoy it.

Throughout the years of intermittently living in Mexico she had studied esoteric teachings, shamanism, energy healing, myofascial release therapy, and various other healing techniques and worked throughout the world in this arena. She stayed with her daughter when she came back from her adventures, which was where she found herself now.

Once she had been referred to as a modern medicine woman, another time a Donna Reed-type medicine woman and a mystic of sorts. It surprised her to hear herself being described in these ways, as she did not feel strongly enough about herself to think she embodied those descriptions. Yes, she was intuitive and a healer, but those were strong words with which she was being associated. Those powerful terms carried a lot of weight, with an undertone of responsibility. At the time, she just smiled and thought about what those depictions really meant.

She had never put a label on herself, nor on what she knew, so to hear inimitable labels coming from someone else was strange to her. She had to think about those expressions for some time before they began to grow on her. It wasn't until later that she decided she was a healer and intuitive, and her perception of herself started to shift. She now appreciated what the words meant and the compliments they represented.

Not only did her grandchildren call her Gum Gum, but even some adults addressed her by that nickname. It came on her originally by her granddaughter, Charlie. Against her daughter's wishes, she would give Charlie gum when she was a young toddler. When she would visit the house, her granddaughter would run up to her saying, "gum, gum." Charlie could not say "grandmother" at the time, so Gum Gum stuck and became her new family name.

Initially when she realized that Gum Gum was going to be her moniker instead of Grandma, she didn't much care for the silly name. The picture that came to her mind was of an old, toothless woman living in the woods in an old cabin. Throughout the years, however, she became accustomed to it and liked that there was a story behind the unique name. Many people, upon hearing the children call her Gum Gum, asked how that nickname came to be hers. Therefore, the story of Gum Gum came to be told repeatedly in fun by her family to others. The name was hers and she wore it well.

★★★

This day on the treadmill, she was mulling over how to write her story. She had hit an impasse on how to go about it, or even how to begin, for that matter. She had been waiting four days for the answer to come to her. She considered the exercise on the treadmill to be her meditation, as insights and answers often came to her in this way.

She put her headphones on and selected the music that took her away from the thoughts in her head and from herself. As always, her usual method was to lightly hold the quandary or issue in her mind and let it expand in its own way.

She was fortunate today, as a vision of a book slowly took form right in front of her eyes. She wasn't quite sure what to make of the vision at first, but she could see that it certainly was a book. Still looking at the image, she noticed a hazy word on the cover. Watching without intensity, for fear of the vision disappearing, she hoped the letters of the word would become clear enough for her to read and better understand what this meant for her. Slowly, the letters became more distinct and she could almost discern the message. Then, she finally recognized the word; she was excited and perplexed at the same time. She wasn't certain what this vision signified, but it was clearly an answer to the challenge she had been pondering.

She asked herself questions. *It was a book*, yes, but how does this apply to me? *How does the word on the book pertain to me?* It all seemed much like a puzzle to figure out and she didn't much care for puzzles. The one word on the book was *FAIRYTALES*. *Hmmm, a book of fairytales…* trying not to get anxious, she thought, *what do I do with this?*

★★★

She felt a shifting taking place within her, and just as quickly as she could snap her fingers, she knew what the book of fairytales meant for her. The purpose felt like a spark, and then a fire inside of her. That *knowing* inspired her to move forward. Instantly, she knew how she was to write the story over which she had been agonizing; she was to write it like a fairytale. She hadn't thought of that before when she was at an impasse in starting her narrative.

She wasn't quite sure how to transform her story into a fairytale, but an idea began taking form and coming alive in her mind. She grew increasingly more excited the longer she was on the treadmill. The words tumbled into her mind; she was ready to begin writing.

She picked up her old, golden pen, worn from use throughout the years. At one time it was beautiful and vibrant, just as she had been. It was given to her as a gift by her father when she was a young woman. She treasured the special pen and always carried it with her for fear it would be lost if she didn't. She began writing her fairytale.

The Fairytale Begins

One afternoon, she was standing in front of the kitchen sink peeling potatoes for dinner. She was forty-eight years old and was feeling rather well this day. For eleven years, she had been struggling to overcome life-threatening health issues. Her two youngest children were nine and ten years of age, and it helped to keep her focus on them instead of how she felt. She was thinking about her children when out of nowhere, with great force, it felt as though someone had kicked her in the stomach. The feeling hit her so hard that the blood drained from her face as she slumped and doubled over the sink. A person might have thought she had a heart attack or stroke if they saw her lying over the sink that way.

In that instant, she had a vision of a young man about fifteen to seventeen years old walking on the sidewalk that led from the garage to his parent's house. She couldn't help but notice that the boy was walking in an awkward, gangly way that didn't seem quite right. Something was severely wrong with this boy. As she continued to watch this surreal movie in front of her, she saw clearly that although he could walk, the boy's face was expressionless and showed a certain lack of comprehension and awareness. She could see that it took all he had mentally and physically just to walk from the garage to the house. Her daughter, Gina, was pregnant and was due to deliver her first child within the month. She knew that this severely handicapped boy was going to be her first grandchild.

A howl came up from deep inside of her gut and ran through her body like a freight train. "No, this can't be! This can't be!" As the whistle of the train pierced through her heart, she felt as if the world had dropped out from under her; she was swimming in the knowledge of a truth that ripped through her soul for what was to come.

When the movie ended, she laid doubled over the sink unable to move. Even though the vision was over, it was forever inside of her now. She couldn't take back what she had felt and all that she had seen. It was too late; the sorrow and grief were embedded in her soul.

★★★

Finally, she ever so slowly pulled herself up from the sink. Shaking as she walked over to a chair, she sat down and cried tears of agony and despair. She prayed, *oh please, God, don't let this be; don't let this be! What can I do to stop this from coming to fruition?* She continued to sob.

The premonition remained with her, and every day she prayed while still holding onto some thread of hope that she was wrong in her *knowing*. What she had been shown was not something she could tell anyone, least of all her daughter. No, she couldn't tell anyone; this was something she alone would know.

The days wore on, and the birth drew closer. The

weight of this secret and the gut-wrenching pain she felt tore her apart. She continued to pray all the harder. She asked God, *what is the purpose of me knowing that my grandson will be handicapped if I can't change it? Or if there is a way for me to change this outcome, please, show me.*

She didn't receive an answer to her question. She didn't know it at the time, but twenty years would pass before she would receive an answer. Therefore, she chose to believe the premonition was intended to prepare her in some way for what was about to become a reality. There wasn't anything that she didn't run through her mind in those weeks before her grandson's birth, in the hopes of lifting the anguish she felt. She tried to pretend that everything was fine with her.

Special Delivery

The day came for her grandson's birth, as her daughter, Gina, was in labor. She was sitting in the hospital waiting room with her two youngest children, whom had come to the hospital with their father. The kids brought balloons and banners to celebrate the new baby's birth. As she sat there looking around the room at the wonderful decorations and gifts, she felt hopeful for the first time in weeks. She noticed all the feelings of anguish and despair were leaving her; she hardly felt them at all in this moment. This seemed curious to her, but she was happy to have those awful feelings subside. *Maybe it was a good sign, maybe everything would be alright,* she thought hopefully.

As her daughter's labor wore on, it seemed to her that it was lasting excessively long. *Thirty-six hours is much too long to be in labor,* she thought. She felt that the doctor should be called back in to assess the situation, and even suggested this to her daughter a few times, but Gina and the nurses didn't seem too concerned about the length of time the delivery was taking. At this point, she felt as though her hands were tied and there was nothing she could do. She thought, *maybe I'm here just to be of support to Gina.* She didn't have strong enough feelings to force the issue, nor did she feel as though she was there to change the outcome in any way.

As she sat in the waiting room, it seemed strange to her that she felt numb, somehow disconnected from the eventful happenings. Her feelings and emotions were anesthetized in some way during what should be a jovial occasion and she felt robbed of the happy experience she should be sharing with her family. Yes, the bad feelings were gone, but she wanted the good ones back.

The thought came to her that this period during the labor was the stillpoint of her seeing–the resting place that falls after the ending of one thing but before the beginning of another–and she was witness to it. While she felt deprived of these joyous feelings, not having them actually put her in a place of neutrality; a place where she could stand back and see the whole picture as it unfolded. All emotions had been wiped from her mind as she sat in this objectivity, allowing her to be strong amidst the unfolding of the coming events. Inside herself, she waited.

On Sunday, March 23, 1997 at 1:08 am, her grandson, Brady, came into this world stillborn. She didn't know this at the time, nor did Brady's parents. At the time he was born, the family didn't have knowledge of this fact, as the stillborn baby was immediately taken away into another hospital room.

She left her daughter's bedside and walked out into the hallway. As she was walking down the corridor she saw a glass window to her left, and like most people would do, she looked through it. What she saw jolted her and brought her to a full stop. As she stood there looking through the window, she saw the newborn, Brady, laying on a table while a doctor was trying to resuscitate him. The doctor picked up one of his little baby arms by the hand, held it in the air, and let go of it… the newborn's lifeless arm fell silently down onto the table. She held her breath in the silent falling of his tiny, limp arm. Witnessing this act left a deep and lasting impression on her. The image was like a snapshot in her mind that she would never forget. Unable to form words or thoughts, she stood there watching the scene as though she were trapped in a living nightmare.

As doctors and nurses continued to work on Brady, she just stood there alone. Finally, after several minutes, the doctors brought the newborn back to life; she saw that Brady was alive. The breath that she had been holding released, and the relief that she felt spread throughout her being. She said to herself, *everything will be alright now.*

When the pediatrician finally arrived at the hospital, he went straight into the room to examine the "bad baby", as the other doctors were referring to the newborn by now. The pediatrician did all that he could for him.

The pediatrician was a friend of hers, and as he noticed

her standing in the hallway, he went out into the corridor to speak with her. Over the course of their conversation, it came up that her grandson had been stillborn. He explained that he was not made aware of the circumstances surrounding Brady's delivery when the hospital staff called him out to care for the baby in distress. Therefore, precious time had been lost in assessing Brady's needs and acting on them. After the conversation, the pediatrician had a better understanding of what had taken place; he returned to continue administering tests and subsequent treatments on her grandson.

She went back to her daughter's birthing room. The family all waited together for someone to bring the baby boy to her daughter and son-in-law. As they anxiously waited for a nurse to bring the baby in, she decided not to tell them of what she had seen—Brady was alive and that was all that mattered. There were no thoughts of anything being wrong; the family only felt the joy of this new baby who had just arrived in the world and in their lives. A nurse wheeled a small Plexiglass box into the room with the sweet baby inside. As she sat there watching her daughter and son-in-law gaze at the baby whom they were not allowed to hold, it appeared that they were fine, and their son was too. They were just like every other happy couple with a new baby.

She had wistfully forgotten all that she *knew* before his birth. While watching the happiness of this new family, she was pulled into the beauty of the scene. Despite the numb, impartial state that she was still in, she saw the magnificence of it, and that was enough for her.

After a brief visit with his parents and grandparents,

Brady was quickly removed from the birthing room. All that had been shared was that the newborn needed more care—no other information was given. At the time, she thought it odd, but still assumed that everything would be alright now.

Shortly afterwards, the pediatrician entered her daughter's room and informed the concerned family that the newborn was being life-flighted to a larger hospital because Brady required specialized care. This hospital had a neonatal intensive care unit (NICU), which was best suited to care for him. Suddenly, the air in the room went flat, and just like a balloon it left everyone deflated.

She could not wrap her mind around the fact that there was something far more wrong with Brady than what anyone had been told; he was a healthy eight and a half pounds, after all. She was still in that numb, neutral state where she could only think from one moment to the next; she was unable to think ahead yet couldn't see behind that moment either.

In hindsight, she realized that if anyone had known the seriousness of the baby's situation and what reality awaited them, they would have been crushed by the overwhelming information being given at one time—that knowledge would have devastated them. As it was, the information came gradually, over a month, while Brady was in the NICU.

Angels in the Room

The next day, Gina was well enough to leave the hospital, so her and Billy wanted to see their baby in the NICU. She rode with her daughter and son-in-law to the larger hospital where Brady was being cared for. As the small family group walked toward the building, she sensed and felt how the three of them fell into a quiet, hushed mood. She thought it came from not knowing what to expect, and yet there was a hint of excitement behind the idea of seeing the baby.

As they walked through the doors into the hospital, the gnawing feeling became palpable as it hung in the air. Looking through a window, the three of them could see the newborn lying in a Plexiglass incubator bed. They were not permitted to hold the baby; the resident doctor explained to the family that Brady was at risk of further damage and his condition was too fragile to risk taking him out of his special crib. The quiet, hushed tone persisted as they continued to stare through the glass at the motionless newborn.

★★★

They could see Brady was in a medically induced coma, and as the three of them stood there, they began to come out of the hypnotized state they had been experiencing since his birth. Questions began rising to the surface, but very little information was given to them; the NICU doctors were still assessing Brady's condition. The family didn't understand what had happened to the newborn; Brady had seemed like a healthy baby when he left his parents' side. The three of them soon learned that his brain had begun to swell during the life-flight to the larger hospital. There was no telling what was wrong with their baby.

As they left, she felt somewhat hopeful, but only in the sense that Brady was still alive. She knew his condition was dire, but maybe the situation wouldn't be as bad as they feared. After all, the doctors hadn't pointedly said anything worse to them beyond Brady's condition being critical. She comforted herself with that thought as they were leaving the hospital to go home.

She went to the NICU every day with Gina, Billy, and Brady's other grandparents. Each time, they all hoped for more information on the baby's condition. Nonetheless, no answers were given—the hospital staff was still evaluating his condition. The family was becoming frustrated and scared as their questions about the newborn remained unanswered. The days were all a blur, and time stood still for her and her daughter.

After a week had passed, the doctors finally called a family meeting. She and the family members went into the small, but comfortable, hospital conference room where the medical team would join them. As she sat there, looking around the room at the other people, she could see in everyone's faces that they were apprehensive and quiet in their demeanor and thoughts—herself included.

She could tell this assembly was planned ahead of time by the doctors. The meeting would be significant in its importance as to how it pertained to Brady and the entire family. The worst part was waiting for the doctors to come into the meeting room; neither she nor anyone else knew what to say to each other. The room was silent. They were on a flight that wanted to land, but were in a holding pattern until otherwise notified.

Finally, a neurologist, a resident, and a NICU attending physician all came into the room along with two other people—a social worker for her family and a case manager for Brady. The team sat down. Instantly she knew this wasn't good; the fact that five specialists—not one—were suddenly involved brought her to attention. The medical team very gently explained that the newborn had sustained a birth injury and the doctors didn't know to what extent the damage would be at this point. All they knew was that the impairment would be severe because his organs had shut down from brain swelling. The doctors did not expect Brady to live for very long. The shoe had finally dropped, and it dropped hard on her and her family. The doctors suggested that Brady be baptized, and Last Rites given as soon as possible. She and the family took in all that had been said; some words came, but there were few. The doctors left once everything they wanted to articulate had been said. She just sat there, as did the others, stunned by what had just been revealed to them.

★★★

She didn't react, as she sat there watching Gina and Billy. Like her, she felt that they were both in a state of extreme emotional balance; they had somehow been moved into this frame of mind to enable them to do what was necessary in the moment. In this state, she and the others were only living in the *now* and acting and reacting in that moment. There were no thoughts cluttering the mind or emotions running around like wild horses. All the feelings and thoughts regarding the possibility of losing the newborn were present, but she felt her family had been protected in this unseen way in order to get through it.

On Easter Sunday, March 30th, 1997, seven days after Brady was born, she, Gina, Billy, the other grandparents, and Brady's aunts and uncles all gathered in a private room in the hospital. Her grandson, Brady, was brought into the room and handed to Gina to hold, as he remained in a coma-like state. She watched as Billy and Gina stood side by side. Gina was holding the baby and Billy ever so gently rested his hand on Brady's tiny head.

A minister entered the room and stood in front of Gina, Billy and the baby. From her perspective, she could not see Brady nestled between his parents. She thought, *if no one knew any different, they would have thought Gina and Billy were getting married.* She found it odd to have such a thought at this particular moment. She liked how this perspective served as a reminder to her of how much perceptions can be colored by appearances. She quietly moved to the other side of the room where she could see Brady and be closer to him and his parents.

There was something nagging at her about the fact that Last Rites were being given to her grandson. She searched inside herself for the reason it was bothering her. She realized it was as though she was saying, okay, *I accept the fact that this baby will die,* as if it was already set in stone.

She did not like that thought at all; in her mind, nothing is ever set in stone. However, what she thought didn't matter in the end.

While she stood there, she noticed it wasn't death that she felt in the room. Instead, what she felt in the room was the lovely, pure, fragrant perfume of angels gathering. The scent of fragrant, angelic perfume grew increasingly stronger, and as the aroma moved throughout the space, the angels' presence sent chills running up and down her spine and throughout her entire body.

Her eyes welled up with tears and she knew then that her grandson had been blessed. Brady was being held in the arms of the angels that had intervened on his behalf. She served as a witness to this extraordinary presence in the gathering room. She knew that somehow, although she didn't know how, he was going to make it.

Fighting for Life

Every day for a month, the family drove up to the hospital. Information about the baby's condition was dribbled out to them over the course of that timespan. Brady was fragile and clinging to life the best he could. She thought, *the angels, their prayers, and their love were the only things that kept Brady earthbound.*

There was one thing she had forgotten–Brady was a warrior; not only do warriors fight, but if they have reason to, they fight even harder. Brady had his own reason to fight. Neither she nor the others were privy to his reason;

it was only through the years that she, Gina, Billy, and the rest of the family came to realize the truth of why Brady was in their lives.

★★★

During one of their visits to the hospital her daughter asked the question, "when can we take Brady home?" Gina was told that she could take him home after spending two nights at the hospital caring for her special newborn.

Brady could not suck or swallow, so a nasal gastric feeding tube was inserted through his nose while he was in the NICU. Brady's formula and medications were fed through this N-G tube. She had never seen anyone being fed that way before and wondered if tubes sliding down his nose and throat would be painful. She came to the conclusion that it must at least be uncomfortable if it didn't hurt. Gina decided that a gastric feeding tube should be surgically placed into Brady's stomach before taking him home.

Several days before Brady was to finally leave the hospital, another family meeting was called by the doctors. Everyone went into the conference room just as they had done before and waited for the professional team to arrive. She looked around the room at her family and thought, *we are all in this together. No matter what is said to us, we know that there is more to this...more than what we can see.*

The attending physician, the resident, the social worker, and the case manager all came into the meeting room and sat down. She and the family very intently looked at the doctor, waiting for him to start. In her opinion, it took him too long to get his thoughts together. *Maybe he didn't know how to approach the family in a situation like this. What role did the others have here?* She could feel herself becoming agitated with the medical team. She wondered, *did the doctor really do the best he could for her grandson? What did the social worker and case worker think they were going to do for them?* These were all thoughts that moved through her mind as she sat there waiting for him to begin.

The doctor began talking, and as he did, she felt as though he sounded rather cold. While he explained that he didn't mean to sound apathetic, she still perceived him as coming off cold and very callous. She and the rest of her family were listening and totally focused on what the doctor was telling them. It was as though they were sitting in a bubble and all other sounds outside of the bubble ceased to exist.

The first thing the doctor said to her and her family was, "I am going to give you a list of words that will be associated with your son. Words that you will be hearing said by others. Traumatic brain injury. Swallowing disorders. Disabled. Retarded. Handicapped. Spastic quadriplegic. Cortically blind. Hearing impaired or deaf. Cerebral palsy. Epilepsy." The doctor continued, "your son has been compromised, and I don't expect him to live longer than a couple of months after he is taken home." After all of this had been conveyed, she and the others were stunned and remained quiet.

She understood all the words, but they seemed outside of her, as though they were suspended in midair before her. No one spoke; she assumed that they too were stuck in this odd place of comprehending everything, but not at the extreme emotional level that the doctor was accustomed to witnessing. She now realized why the social worker and case manager were included. They were there to handle the emotions that distressed families display once given this kind of disturbing news. She also realized that she, Gina, Billy, and the other family members were all reacting, or rather not reacting, in the same manner; everyone was very emotionally balanced. Gina and Billy asked questions, and so did she–inquiries that were appropriate and pertained to Brady's diagnosis and prognosis.

She thought to herself, *how funny that even though the doctor said all those words and made it very clear that Brady would die, it does not seem like the truth. Who thinks something like that when given tragic news? Am I in denial, is my whole family in denial?* She softly let the thought go, assuming it to be inconsequential in the scheme of things. It was not trivial to the doctor, the social worker, or the case manager, she was to find out later. At a different family meeting, the doctor and social worker were concerned that the family hadn't yet accepted Brady's prognosis; they believed that her family was in denial because they reacted differently than others.

No one on the medical team comprehended that they wouldn't allow heartbreak to overcome their family during this important gathering. Billy very quickly expressed to the doctor and social worker that they wanted to make the best use of everyone's time by remaining calm and asking questions. Just because they were not overly emotional with the physicians and specialists did not mean that her family didn't breakdown emotionally upon returning home. She was very proud that her son-in-law had spoken up and set the medical team straight regarding her family's emotional health.

Another reason Billy's outspokenness pleased her was that she and her family were becoming very frustrated by the staff's inconsiderate comings and goings throughout the crucial discussion. Billy, Gina, her, and the others had questions and wanted to continue with the meeting rather than talk about their emotional needs; there were more important issues at hand to deal with.

They were approaching the day that Brady could go home. The gastroenterologist surgically placed a gastric feeding tube in Brady's stomach; he was to be fed in the same manner as with the nasal tube, this tube was just in a different place. Gina quickly learned how to feed, suction, and care for her baby. Even though he required around the clock care, her daughter did so well her first night that a second night in the hospital was not required for him to leave. After thirty days in the hospital, Gina and Billy could now take their son home.

She was feeling edgy and nervous as they drove up to the hospital to finally pick up their bundle of joy. They were going to bring home this little, fragile baby boy that no one expected to live; she was scared. She was afraid that she would make a mistake and worsen Brady's condition; it was a feeling that she couldn't shake.

She wondered if Gina and Billy were feeling the same way that she was; she didn't ask, but assumed they probably were. *How could they not feel afraid, yet happy they were going to bring their baby boy home?*

After the family arrived at the hospital, they went directly to the critical care unit. Everything was prepared

157

for Brady to leave and be with his family. Once again, instructions were given on how to feed and care for the frail baby. The doctor reminded the family, one final time, that their delicate newborn might only live for a month or two. She heard what the doctor said but didn't entertain the thought of her grandson dying. She could feel the fragileness of this new infant and the weighted responsibility of this little life now being in their hands. She never experienced a fear such as this before; a fear of holding the life of another in her hands—especially a fragile baby that could die at any moment.

She could feel how loosely Brady's life hung in the balance and that it wouldn't take much to tip the scales in the wrong direction. As afraid as the three of them were, there was happiness in them as well, because now Brady was coming home. All the love that they carried inside of them could now be shared and given to him. Her family didn't know what lied ahead, nor did they think about it; they just bravely welcomed Brady into their hearts and carried him home.

Stay Just a Little While Longer

She lived seven houses away from her daughter, just up the block. Both her and her daughter's houses overlooked a lovely lake in a quiet little borough of approximately seven hundred residents. The closest metropolitan cities were two hours south and west of where she lived, an especially long drive in an emergency situation. She was happy that all she had to do was walk down the street—it was extremely convenient for her. She was grateful for the close proximity that made it so much easier to help her daughter; every day she would walk to Gina's house to help her care for Brady.

Her firstborn, Gina, was twenty-eight years old. As she watched her daughter care for Brady, she realized she was a very capable, strong woman. Gina was wise beyond her years and always had been; even when she was a young girl it seemed as though she was an old soul. These characteristics now became apparent in the way Gina very swiftly had all the vulnerable boy's needs under control; it was as though she was born for mothering a special baby. Although no one would ever consciously choose a situation like this, as she looked around at her daughter and the situation it seemed to her that there was something bigger going on than any of them knew.

Brady came home with oxygen, twenty-four-hour tube feedings, medications (for reflux and seizures), and in need of constant suctioning of his nose and mouth for mucus that he couldn't swallow. A nurse was quickly brought in to work eight-hour night shifts, seven days a week, so Gina could sleep during the night. Brady needed nonstop care and it was up to her and Gina to do so during the day and evening.

One afternoon, soon after Brady came home, Gina and Billy had left to do some shopping. She went into her grandson's room, picked him up as gently as she could, and snuggled him deeper into his blanket. She didn't want to cause him any more pain than he was already experiencing from the brain swelling and his other physical issues. Holding her grandson in her arms, she sat down in the beige wooden leather glider chair. She thought it was better than a typical rocking chair, as this glider was smoother and moved effortlessly back and forth. While she was rocking Brady, she considered how she was most frightened during the times she was alone with her grandson. When Gina and Billy were home, the three of them acted together as a support system for each other in the event that something happened to Brady, but now they were elsewhere.

Even though she felt fearful, she continued to rock and sing him *Mocking Bird,* along with other sweet lullabies. She could feel her grandson's pain and how scared he was, so she drew him even closer to her body. She herself was afraid of the fragile baby dying in her arms when she was alone with him; she didn't know how she could bear it if he died in her arms. While she held and kissed him, she told Brady not to do anything silly, like leave. In those moments, she gave him all the love and strength she had to keep him going just a little while longer. "Just a little while longer," she said to her fragile grandson; "you just need to stay with us a little while longer." A little while longer was to her, and to his parents, one minute at a time.

A little while longer turned into longer and longer, as Brady continued to stay with her family. Every time she was with her grandson she would thank God for helping him live another hour. Sometimes, she wondered if she had done the right thing by hanging on to him so tightly and trying desperately to keep him here. She knew that her fragile grandson was in severe pain most of the time since he cried nonstop. She wondered, *how long can he bear that kind of pain before he gives up?* She never ceased trying to hold on to him though, even with the thoughts she had. Letting Brady go didn't seem to be an option.

★★★

During the two months following his homecoming, there were two heart-wrenching emergency trips to the local ER, which sent Brady to a children's hospital for aspiration pneumonia.

The days marched on, and soon the two-month lifespan Brady had been given fell into the distance as he continued to persevere. Each day that passed was a miracle in and of itself–Brady was still with them. He remained in a fragile state, but he had a will unlike no other to survive.

Feelings

A few months had passed when she began to notice feelings of anger towards her daughter rising to the surface. These sentiments would come and go, and she couldn't make any sense of the way she was feeling. She knew there wasn't any reason for her to feel that way; her daughter had done nothing wrong. She allowed the feelings to come and just observed the emotions to see if a reason for them would show itself.

Over the course of three weeks, the root of this attitude eventually became clear. She was mad at her daughter because she didn't change doctors during her pregnancy. She had asked Gina on multiple occasions to switch Ob-

Gyns due to some disturbing stories she heard about the doctor. Each time she brought it up, her daughter told her in a very calm manner that she didn't feel as though she needed to change physicians and wasn't interested in doing so. She finally let it drop and decided not to mention it anymore. The plaguing feeling that *Brady's life would have been different if Gina had changed doctors* continued to rear its ugly head.

She didn't reveal to Gina the feelings that she was experiencing, as she decided it was unnecessary to add anything further to the situation in her daughter's life. She disliked having these feelings because the incident was in the past and it could no longer be changed; it was what it was. She needed to work this out herself, and work it out quickly, at that. She certainly did not want this to interfere with their relationship, especially with all the changes taking place in their lives. Not only did she need to be there for her daughter, but she needed to be in the right frame of mind.

She grappled with how to shift herself out of these thoughts and emotions, as she knew in her mind that it wasn't right thinking. She didn't like the anger she experienced when she was around her daughter and knew that somehow, she had to accept Gina's decision. Even though she would give herself a good talking to when the feelings surfaced, it didn't seem to work.

It took some time before clarity came and she could make peace with these feelings; she finally realized the issue was actually with herself all along. She saw several things, not just one thing, about herself; she realized that her ego was hurt because it wanted to control everything and was afraid of letting go. She recognized that while her girl was a grown woman, she still wanted to control her daughter and tell her what to do. She was mad at Gina because she hadn't listened and done as her mother told.

★★★

She was drawn back to the beginning, before Brady was born...back to when she had the premonition. As that occurred, she realized several things–she had *seen* that her grandson would be severely handicapped. While Gina was in labor she didn't feel guided to act upon that knowledge; in fact, at that time she was in an odd state of extreme neutrality, a holding pattern, as though she was not meant to do anything but wait. It wasn't her place to dictate to her daughter what she was to do, and it wasn't her place to control the outcome of Brady's birth. She knew that she had high respect for Gina; the wisdom her daughter possessed, and the judgment calls she had made through-out her life, were above reproach. She *saw* that Gina had not been guided to change doctors or make any decisions other than those which she made before and during her labor–she had done exactly what she was meant to do.

This had all been orchestrated before Brady was even born. He was the star of this grand play, and they were the supporting actors in his play.

The truth behind her feelings came to the surface as if they stood in front of her; finally, there was no more ar-guing with herself or being angry with her daughter. All the emotions that she had carried within her began to dis-solve and drift away; she felt her body respond to the truth with its own deep release, as if her body also acknowledged the truth. She couldn't articulate or put into words the shifts taking place inside of her. All she knew was that when she looked at both of their actions, and the way they felt before and during Brady's birth, she recognized that she and Gina did exactly what they were meant to do—which was nothing. The 'what ifs' didn't stop overnight, though; it took her several weeks to fully integrate this change in her perception.

She even questioned herself about whether it was her mind's way of somehow justifying her own feelings of guilt over not changing the outcome of Brady's birth and wanting to blame someone else—mainly her daughter. *Was it her mind's inability to wrap itself around the fact that this happened, and it shouldn't have?* Some would think so, she thought to herself. She knew the truth when she saw it though, and she also knew that her perception shift had come from a source higher than her own.

The Love Connection

It wasn't until twenty years later that she discovered the reason for the *knowing* of Brady's state before he was born as she read it in his journal entries. When she read what he wrote, it was like the last piece to a puzzle fell into place; it brought tears to her eyes. After all those years, she finally received an answer as to why...why Brady had always been able to connect with her, his grandmother.

When she read Brady's journal, she could feel him standing beside her; his presence was strong and filled with love. Her grandson was there to help her again and give her what she needed at the time. The love she felt for him came up in tears–she missed him so. If only she could hug him, touch him in the physical; but even she knew that wasn't possible. She felt his love come through to her, and that was enough.

She read in his journal that Brady had connected to her before his birth in order to establish a link with her, a heartbridge. It was essential that he have a link with someone to be able to connect in a nonphysical way after he was born. Brady needed someone he could go to, someone whom could hear and see him when he needed comfort or help. He wanted someone to speak to and communicate through.

It was an unexpected and wonderful blessing to learn Brady's reason for connecting to her, and the blessing had come in a surprising way. She sat there for a while, wrapped up in his love, and overwhelmed with happiness over the gift Brady had just given her. Even after all these years, her grandson was still with her when she needed him; it absolutely boggled her mind to think how this was at all conceivable. She was thankful that it was possible to go beyond time, space, and the physical to create a heartbridge.

Acceptance and Resiliency

When Brady was around five months old, Gina called her in to witness how the baby boy was attempting to lift his head. This was a delayed milestone, but something to be excited about nonetheless. The two of them kept it a secret for fear of others thinking that they were just imagining Brady doing what they hoped to see.

Another month passed. She went into Brady's room as he was lying in his crib and saw his body move in a strange way that she had never seen before; she had been around him long enough to know that this movement didn't look right. At first, Brady's knees pulled up to his chest, then his body straightened and went stiff. The incident only lasted for a few seconds, but she still thought it odd. Gina came into the room a few minutes after the strange movement took place, so she described to her daughter what she had witnessed. Gina told her that yes, she had seen similar unusual movements also. Neither one of them knew what to make of these episodes; they were so fleeting that they decided to just keep an eye on it for the time being.

Within a week's time, these unusual movements grew intensely worse; Brady now cried during these spells and collapsed in exhaustion afterwards. Arrangements were made to take him to see a neurologist at the children's hospital in Pittsburgh. As she pushed her grandson through the facility, she was startled in a mind-altering way. She saw children in the lobby, children in the hallways, children in the elevator, and children in the doctor's waiting room. She had never seen so many children, from babies to young teens, in such a concentrated area before. They had every physical deformity and condition imaginable; she couldn't help but look at them and let her heart open up to them. It wasn't something she could easily explain–this feeling fell outside the physical realm of description.

She was amazed at the seemingly calm acceptance and resiliency of the children. They had various and severe conditions to deal with, and she was profoundly affected by their courage and bravery in facing their own unique situations. Beautiful, innocent children who had been dealt a bad hand, yet despite everything, had found a way to rise above it.

The thought crossed her mind, *if she had never seen so many children like this before, then most people probably hadn't either. If they did see this many challenged kids together, would it affect them the same way it did her? Would it change them in a most subtle way like it did her? She hoped it would.* These thoughts crossed her mind every time she went to the children's hospital. She contemplated things like this when she would see something that startled her enough to stop and open her heart. *Would other people perceive the same thing that she did? If they did,* she thought, *it would begin to change the world in how people looked at each other. Hearts couldn't help but open up, and that's when change would begin.*

Once Brady's neurology appointment had ended, the four of them headed home. In the car ride back, they discussed Brady's diagnosis and prognosis; Brady was experiencing seizures called *infantile* spasms, which resembled a jackknife to her. The doctor increased Brady's seizure medication. There was no way for the neurologist to know if Brady would develop long term epilepsy, but it was a real possibility given the severe brain trauma he had sustained during the birthing process.

The increase in seizure medication helped very little and Brady continued to have infantile spasms. It was difficult and painful for her and the family to watch the jackknife-like seizures that came on fast and hard. The look she saw in Brady's eyes was one of, "what the hell is going on here?" A lost look that said he didn't understand what or why his body was moving like this; a look of horror and of no control over what was happening to him. He would cry as if he was in excruciating pain. The neurologist informed her and the family that Brady wasn't in any pain, but they all knew better. Once the seizures were over, she could see that the episodes exhausted Brady; she would hold and soothe him the best she could, and so did his mother and father. Sometimes he was already in her arms when he would seize, and she only hoped that they would get him stabilized quickly. Having these seizures was taking too much out of him; Brady was continually losing what little progress he had made. He was still alive, and they wanted to keep him alive.

Months later, Brady was placed in an experimental seizure drug trial. Over a few months' time, his seizure activity was cut in half and gradually disappeared. They subsided completely when he was around two years old, which was a godsend because the seizure medication trial was discontinued at the hospital almost simultaneously.

Going in Search of Help

Brady was about six months old when she suggested to her daughter that they should take him to a specialist in New England whose specialty was orthomolecular biochemistry medicine. This expert had been her doctor for eleven years and had quite literally saved her life when she was thirty-nine years old. She held him in very high regard and deeply respected how his specialized practice had helped her. She felt that if anyone could help Brady, it would be this doctor. As soon as she called the specialist and filled him in on Brady's condition, he immediately set up an appointment for her grandson.

She helped her daughter load up a customized van that they had borrowed for the trip. This was a long trip to take Brady on—the specialist was six hundred and fifty miles away. He was still very fragile and required oxygen and suctioning; both she and her daughter were nervous about traveling that far with him but felt that visiting this doctor was the best thing for Brady. They pushed aside their fears and trusted that they would make it there and back with him no worse off than his current condition. Hopefully, the doctor would be able to help stabilize his health.

While the road trip started without issues, it wasn't more than a couple of hours into the drive when Brady began throwing up more than formula. He was vomiting a dark reddish-brown liquid that neither of them recognized, but they continued to drive; they had to—they were committed now. It turned out to be something called *coffee grounds,* a term used to describe old blood from acid reflux. There was yet another challenge to face with Brady.

The specialist was very kind and sympathetic towards her grandson's condition and took his time to evaluate him and his needs. When he was finished, the expert gave Gina a list of nutritional supplements tailored just for Brady; some vitamins were to help the brain swelling, while the remaining vitamins were for various other needs. Throughout the years, Brady's nutritional supplements mirrored his needs as they changed. As such, she and Gina continued to drive him to the specialist's office in New Hampshire every six months until he was strong enough to only require an annual visit.

Other than the severe acid reflux arising, they returned home without serious complications; she was relieved they had made the return trip without a serious health crisis occurring. In her mind it was a successful trip and now she and her daughter could get to work implementing Brady's new nutritional supplement regimen. At first, they combined Brady's supplements with his baby formula; occasionally when he was stronger they would mix the vitamins into blended foods. She and her daughter were very religious about making sure Brady received all his nutritional supplements on a daily basis; this was the only way in which she felt she could help in some small way to improve his condition. Otherwise, she felt helpless; at least in making sure Brady had his supplements she was taking a positive step in the right direction for his healing.

Giving Brady the large number of vitamins was very difficult; they would sometimes settle in the baby formula as it sat in the feed pump bag and tubing, so she or Gina would find the blockage and fix it. Unclogging the tubing was especially difficult if the obstruction was found to be in the G-tube in his abdomen. Billy brought home an eight-inch long piece of malleable copper wire for Gina or her to ever so slowly and tenderly fish down inside of Brady's feeding tube to unclog it. Under no circumstances was anyone else allowed to unblock the tube in this manner. In fact, the copper wire was even hidden from the nursing staff.

The nutritional supplements helped her grandson over the course of many years. What this specialist did for him was considered by Brady's parents to be his first miracle. The frail baby boy had been on oxygen twenty-four hours a day, seven days a week, since his birth. At one point, ear, nose, and throat doctors pushed Billy and Gina to give Brady a tracheotomy. The specialist, however, told her daughter to give him one tablet of Sudafed a day. After they arrived home, Gina did just that; Brady was taken off oxygen within thirty-six hours of his first two doses of Sudafed. From then on, Brady only required oxygen when he was sick, and sometimes not even then.

★★★

Two and a half years had passed; during that time, she and her daughter continued to search for cutting-edge medical and alternative therapy treatments with the hope of finding some way to improve Brady's health and bring him more comfort. In those years, she and her daughter took Brady for hyperbaric oxygen therapy (HBOT). Although the doctors did not recommend they try this type of treatment on Brady, her daughter had researched HBOT and decided there was nothing to lose by trying it. The idea was to get more oxygen to his brain and body.

She felt the HBOT did help Brady, but it was in ways that might have been undetectable to the human eye. What she later read in his journal confirmed her thoughts, and she knew he was still laughing about her episode in the tank. This made all the numerous dives they took, and her panic attack in the small hyperbaric tank, worthwhile. When she read in his journal, *"in that moment, I knew that my mind had made a connection of recognition that these clubs were really my arms,"* waves of shivers vibrated throughout her body. At that moment she knew this was his way of communicating to her that hyperbaric oxygen therapy did make a difference. Tears filled her eyes as her heart was struck by an exuberant charge that circulated throughout her being while she stood in the wonderment of it all.

Grieving for Brady

Billy and Gina lived in a one-hundred-year-old house, but the view of the lake was spectacular and made up for the age of the home. The nursery was bright and sunny, decorated in yellow and white striped wallpaper, and only one-hundred square feet in size. This was not nearly enough space for baby furniture, medical equipment, two caregivers, and Brady.

Not only was the climb up the steep steps hard for

some of the staff, but the layout of the house also made it difficult for her daughter and son-in-law to care for their special baby and maintain some resemblance of a family life. Every time she went to Gina's house there were any number of nurses in the living area, which couldn't be helped. Life revolved around Brady, and there was no privacy whatsoever for Gina and her husband. She could hear everything that went on in their home—Brady, the nurse, the medical equipment; it didn't matter what it was, she could hear it all.

The Victorian house was also becoming too small for the growing family. She had been concerned that her daughter would not have more children for fear that something would go wrong again. Although Gina was apprehensive about have another child, she pushed past the fear and gave birth to a beautiful, healthy baby girl; she was a grandmother again. She now had a new grandbaby to help with. Her granddaughter was a delight and brought hope and happiness to the family when they needed it most.

She knew her daughter was overwhelmed with organizing nurses, caring for Brady sixteen hours a day, constantly taking him to the doctors in Pittsburgh, and now caring for another baby. Her grandson was still very fragile and in the kind of pain that could be felt in his cries.

There was never a moment to just breathe for her daughter. She helped as much as she could to relieve the stress, but even that wasn't enough. She and Gina discussed remodeling the existing house to be more suitable for Brady and his nurses, but in the end an addition and renovation project would be such a massive undertaking for her daughter that she would not, and could not, take on one more thing–she was too overwhelmed as it was.

The search was on for a new home that was better suited for their family's needs. Her daughter found the right house; a home that would give them, Brady, and his nurses some much needed privacy. She was happy that Gina had found the right place, but also a little heartbroken for her. She knew that her daughter had given up the home she loved and was torn about making the move.

She was sad about her daughter's family moving away from their street; she would no longer be able to walk down the sidewalk to see her grandson. However, she knew that Gina had made the decision with everyone's best interest at heart and that it had to be done; she was right about making the decision to move.

Her grandson was four and his little sister was two when her daughter's family moved into their new home. Brady's new bedroom was located on the first floor, down the hall from the kitchen. It was a large bedroom with plenty of space for his medical equipment, wheelchair, shower chair, oxygen concentrator, and everything else he required. The bedroom was big enough for her daughter to buy him a new fully electric hospital bed–it was the Cadillac of medical beds. There was a push-button electric door installed, along with a new heated ramp, that led into Brady's new suite. Not only did the private entry make it easier to take him in and out, but the nurses could come and go without disturbing the family.

Gina designed a bathroom with a wheel-in shower that had a handheld showerhead, so Brady could be bathed every day. There was a separate area that served as a TV room and an office for the nurses to do their reports. In addition, a closet was converted into a small kitchenette to prepare his formula, vitamins, and medications.

She didn't remember much about the move, other than the fact that she noticed the stress levels in the new home had dropped considerably. New routines started to fall into place for Brady and the rest of the household. There was quiet now, where previously there was not. She sensed Brady was enjoying the quietude and seemed a little calmer as well.

Shortly after the move, she began to notice a subtle depression set in. At first, the feeling was fleeting. She wasn't quite sure where the depressed state was originating from or why she was feeling that way; her and her daughter's lives had settled down some and some of the distractions and chaos were gone. Now that everything was more calm, emotions could surface; perhaps that was why this feeling set in.

This sensation came to her increasingly more often until she recognized it for what it was. The feeling was "grieving"; she was grieving for Brady and for the life that he would never be able to have. He would never be able to experience walking through the grass, he would never be able to talk or yell if he wanted to. He would never be able to pick up a fork and eat food from a plate or grab and hold onto a toy by himself. He would never be able to see the stars at night or hear the sound of a puppy's bark. This grieving came up from deep inside of her, but it was a soft, gentle sorrow; a grief that was meant to be heard and felt, but not so much so that it would overwhelm and knock her down. This mourning was a delayed reaction; an emotional reaction that she didn't have at the time of his birth. She thought it funny and odd that it took four years for her emotions to catch up with her. The delay was understandable in a way, though, considering that all their time was spent caring for Brady and keeping him alive. Keeping him alive was all that mattered to her and his parents these last four years. When he left the hospital, the doctors never thought Brady would live more than a couple of months, and he was still with them after four years. He was alive because of the love and care that they had given him—this she believed without reservation or doubt.

It was now time for her to grieve in her own silent way. She noticed, as she was going through this process, the house grew quieter—this was unusual. She decided to discuss this with her daughter to find out if Gina was going through the same delayed grieving process. She didn't want to upset her daughter by talking about Brady if she wasn't ready, so she approached her very gently. As she began to tell Gina how still the house had become, she could tell that her daughter was open to talking about Brady and his situation. Slowly and hesitantly, she shared with Gina what she herself was going through. She then asked her daughter if she was grieving as well.

She observed a great deal of sadness and grief in her daughter's eyes; the look that crossed over Gina's face was one of deep pain. Her daughter very quietly answered, "yes, how could I not?" The sorrow and agony of a broken heart, which carried through in her daughter's voice, spoke more than words ever could.

No consoling words came from either of them; nothing

could be said that would change a dispirited and heavy heart, and they both knew it. A quiet understanding moved between them as her and her daughter accepted where they both were emotionally and what they were going through; the bond between the two of them was one of spirit and love. This inner connection was what held them up and how they comforted each other.

She, her daughter, and her son-in-law moved through their grief, each in their own silent way. Over time it lifted, just as most things do, if you experience them without resistance. There came to be a certain acceptance regarding what Brady's life would be, so they did the best they could to make it more comfortable and as pain free as possible. They didn't know if Brady even knew who they were; he was silent, sightless, and all the things the doctors said he would be. Discouraging as it was at times, they didn't give up on him.

The Kissing Ritual

As her two youngest children grew to be teenagers, she worked the afternoon shift taking care of Brady for a number of years, as there always seemed to be a shortage of agency nursing care. She enjoyed being with her grandson. Every night after she fed and readied him for bed, she would go into the nurse's office and turn on the TV, play music, or pick out a book. She then went back into Brady's bedroom, picked him up, and carried him into the TV room. She sat down in the rocking chair with him and the two of them would watch television or do whatever she felt Brady wanted to do that evening. Sometimes, it was play comforting music if he didn't feel well; other times, it was lively cartoons that she felt he would want to watch if he was feeling spirited.

She would rock Brady until he fell asleep. Knowing that he was resting comfortably, she didn't want to disturb his peaceful slumber, so she would continue to rock him. He so rarely slept for long periods of time; she wanted to give him as much time as possible to enjoy a deep and untroubled slumber. She continued this tradition until Brady grew too big for her to pick up and carry into the television room.

Wanting to continue their nightly ritual, she considered how to get Brady into the television room with her. She decided that she had just enough strength to pick him up and quickly transfer him to his wheelchair. Once Brady was in his wheelchair, she would push him in the other room, so he could sit beside her. The the two of them would then do what they always did—decide what it was going to be for the evening—TV, music, or a story. It wasn't the same for her anymore, though; she missed rocking Brady. Rocking was their time to cuddle up and feel warm together; to talk to each other and share mind thoughts. Feeling her grandson fall asleep in her arms comforted them both in an unseen way.

★★★

Those early years were filled with trips to the emergency room, the pediatrician's office, and the children's hospital.

At that time, crises of one kind or another were the norm in their lives. Sometimes they would make three trips in a week to the children's hospital, which was two hours away. Brady had a different doctor for each of his health issues. Her daughter never had a minute to herself; in fact, she didn't have a life outside of caring for Brady and his siblings. Gina was lost in a sea of doctor appointments, medical emergencies, nursing schedules, medication schedules, formula orders, therapy sessions, diaper changes, and equipment orders.

During this time, her daughter had delivered her third child; Brady now had a baby brother named Riley. Even though Gina was simultaneously raising two other children and running a household, she still somehow continued to research cutting-edge therapies and doctors in hope of finding anything that might bring Brady more comfort and a better quality of life. Gina never complained, she just did what she had to do with an uncommon strength and courage that maternal figures find within themselves.

There is a natural instinct that comes when a woman has children to protect and care for, unless that instinct has been distorted in some way, through no fault of one's own. Children bring out the courage and strength in women to stand up, persevere, defend, and to save their children if necessary. She knew her daughter carried this basic and natural instinct, and she knew she carried it inside herself too.

During those fifteen years, she was the driver of the caravan; wherever her daughter and Brady went, she went. While she was the driver at times, she was also the helper or nurse. She felt incredibly fortunate to be able to assist in carrying some of the responsibility when it came to taking care of her grandchildren. She was included in all medical and surgical discussions, and if her position was offered or asked for, she was heard. She considered herself privileged to be involved in the decisions for her special grandson.

★★★

During Brady's first seven years of life, he was unable to respond, see, hear, recognize or do. However, there was one thing she did that somehow found its way through to him—when Brady was laying in his bed, she would lean over his face and slowly kiss his forehead, eyes, cheeks, ears, and chin. These were long kisses that said, *I love you*. Anywhere there was a space on his head and face, she kissed it. She kissed him repeatedly and as she did, a glow would begin to appear on his face. The glow would build and expand until his face took on a dazzling, radiant light that engulfed her. Then, she would give Brady her special butterfly kiss as a finishing touch. Any time he looked tired or worn from living in an uncooperative body, she performed this kissing ritual. Even if he was resting comfortably she would do this little tradition, knowing that he would enjoy it even more. She had found the one thing that he was able to respond to and the two of them could have fun with the kissing game together.

Although Brady never laughed or smiled, she knew that he was in there somewhere, and that on some level, he loved the kissing ritual. Through her own experiences many years in the past, she found that if one has any kind of limitation it is important to find out what one is capable of doing outside of that constraint. Once you know what you can do, start from there; at that point of discovering what the new ability or perspective has to offer, experiment with it—but most of all, have fun in the experience.

Miracles Do Happen

Brady was beginning his seventh year of life when his mother found a special neurologist practicing cutting-edge medicine in Florida. The doctor's methods sounded promising and worth looking into, so Gina studied the techniques he used and the types of brain injuries he was treating. After thorough research and a few phone calls to the neurologist, she and her daughter decided to take Brady to Florida for treatment.

The flight arrangements were made, a traveling nurse was chosen, and Brady's siblings were prepared for the hope-filled trip; everything he would need was laid out and planned for. They had never flown with Brady, so every precaution was taken to ensure a safe trip for him and the group.

While navigating through airports and traveling on planes, she and her daughter always had to stay alert and pay close attention to what was occurring in their surroundings. There was much to do and to keep an eye on—care for Brady's younger siblings, make sure the nurse stayed with the group and carried identification, confirm that the suction and feeding pumps were charged and within reach, and ensure everything ran as smoothly as possible for her traveling family.

Going through security could sometimes be a challenge. Inevitably, Brady and his wheelchair would be stopped and isolated to a small glass area to be searched by hand. There were times when security would insist that he be taken alone into a small private room, but that just could not happen; Gina firmly made it clear that he could not be left unattended without a caregiver. She explained that Brady needed to be suctioned, and therefore, airport security would be responsible if the boy choked to death on his own spit while in their hands. It was finally under duress that the airport staff would relent and she, his mother, or the nurse—whoever seemed to be most available in the moment—would go with Brady and the security crew into the pat-down area. A very comprehensive search of him and his wheelchair took place. Once cleared, Brady was able to leave and catch up with the rest of the family waiting outside the checkpoint.

Watching the children, caring for Brady, and making sure all the carry-on bags and equipment bags were with them was stressful, to say the least. Sometimes she noticed that the nurse had disappeared and would ask her daughter where he or she had wandered to; most often it was to the restroom or off for a cigarette break. Once on the plane, everything would quiet down slightly, and she and the nurse would take turns caring for Brady, depending on whose shift it was. It was only on occasion that flying was difficult for her grandson. She sensed that he loved to fly and travel, so for her that made the inconveniences worthwhile.

In an effort to eliminate pressure in Brady's ears during hyperbaric oxygen therapy dives her daughter had tubes put in his ears. She felt the tubes in his ears made flying more bearable for him. Otherwise, taking her oldest grandson places might have been more painful and limiting for him.

She and her daughter checked into their hotel rooms and settled everyone in. All bags were counted to be sure none were missing–especially Brady's. He and the nurse always shared a room, which adjoined to the one that her, Gina, Riley and Charlie all occupied. These room arrangements allowed the nurse to sleep during the daytime while she and Gina cared for Brady and gave them the opportunity to sleep at night while the nurse cared for him in his room. Brady didn't sleep much and required meds and feedings throughout the night.

The next day was Brady's appointment with the neurologist; she didn't know what to expect, or if the doctor's treatment would even help him. In the back of her mind, there had always been the hope of a miracle. As naïve as that sounded, she had dreams in which he was walking and talking with her; it was during those times that she thought it was even more possible for him to be healed and be whole. She would also cry because the memory of the dream wasn't the reality they lived in the wake of day. She was afraid to speak of hope out loud, perhaps it would be jinxed if she did.

Her idea of being whole, in the sense of the physical, may not be the truth of where wholeness lies. She thought about this as they sat in the specialist's waiting room. *Surely it was a part of it, though.* Whether it was or not, she decided that the outcome had not yet been written. Therefore, she would continue to be positive in a slightly detached manner and be open to whatever happened.

She found the neurologist's office on a back street inside an old, two story white house. *Not too impressive,* she thought to herself as she drove into the parking lot; *but you never know about these things…looks can be deceiving.* Her daughter, the nurse, and Brady's siblings were all with her. She and Gina unloaded his wheelchair, assembled it, and transferred him from the car to the chair—a routine they knew well; they all walked inside the building together.

She and the others sat in the reception area and acted as though it were just any other day. It was not like any other day though; their hopes were riding on this visit. What everyone was hoping for, they didn't even know. Any change for Brady was welcome; no conditions or specifics were placed on their hope, nor how it would manifest. As it was finally his turn to see the doctor, the neurologist thoroughly reviewed his medical records and discussed everything with them; he explained how Brady's brain cells were either dead or dormant and showed her and Gina the head scans of his brain.

The practitioner explained what happens when a traumatic brain injury occurs—some brain cells are killed and die, never to be revived; while other brain cells get *bumped* and go to sleep, they are merely dormant. The neurologist's proposed therapy was to increase blood circulation throughout Brady's brain; the greater volume of blood would deliver more oxygen to the dormant cells and, in essence, wake up those that were 'sleeping'.

If his protocol worked it could potentially wake up the

dormant cells, which would allow Brady's development to progress from that point. There was no way of predicting how much or how little this treatment would help him because there was no telling how many dormant cells existed or what functions would be restored. The caveat the neurologist provided didn't bother her or Gina; they were there to give Brady the chance of experiencing a better quality of life than what he had, which at the time was none. Anything was better than nothing, at least in their eyes.

The special doctor pulled a tube of cream out of his jacket; he explained that this medication was called nitroglycerin or nitro-bid, and it was typically used on heart patients to increase blood flow. He rubbed a small amount of the nitro-bid on Brady's arm and the four of them waited for about ten or fifteen minutes to see if any change took place. She watched Brady intensely, wanting to see if she noticed any difference in him; but he showed no visible or measurable signs of response to the medication. The neurologist told her and Gina they could take Brady back to the hotel and return the next day.

As they left the doctor's office, she felt somewhat let down. Old thoughts began to creep back into her mind, thoughts that told her this treatment wouldn't be any different and none of this would help Brady. The tug-of-war between faith and negative acceptance is a hard one to fight. Where is the line drawn that you know when to hope and when to let go and accept? Giving up on someone or something still leaves unresolved emotional pain behind; a slow, unconditional acceptance of "the way things are" is not easy. There is a grieving to pass through in order to get to that point of acceptance. Once that point has been reached, a beautiful grace follows; a feeling of well-being. That's when healing occurs and is what keeps you afloat and sustains you through the hardest of times.

She thought she had already passed though the grieving part three years prior; however, it was evident to her now that there were still some lingering threads which were hanging on and needed to be examined. She had accepted Brady the way he was and had already mourned over that reality. What she was seeing now was a conflict between her deep belief that he would be healed and why *it hadn't manifested in his physical form yet. Why hadn't he been healed in some way?* She asked herself this question as she left the doctor's office.

She had trouble wrapping her mind around inquiries to which she didn't have the answers, so what she did next was what she usually did—she quietly let the question go but held it gently until the answer revealed itself to her. She and her daughter had always trusted in their being guided to do the things for Brady that they felt were to his benefit. All she had now was that trust. She tried her best to stay neutral and unattached to an outcome; there were more doctor visits to follow, so it was too soon to predict anything.

The next day she drove everyone back to the neurologist's office. The doctor asked, "did you notice any changes in Brady after you left yesterday?" They glumly replied that they had not. Just as he had before, the doctor took the tube of nitro-bid out of his pocket and rubbed the cream on Brady's arm. This time he applied the paste twice instead of once. She, Gina, and the doctor all watched Brady intently to see if there were any shifts or changes. The four of them waited and watched for fifteen minutes, and other than more color coming to his face, nothing happened. The doctor ended the session and instructed them to return again the following day.

She drove everyone back to the hotel to get something to eat and suggested that they do a little sight seeing to take their minds off the purpose of them being there. The two younger children needed to get out just as much as her and Gina did; everyone needed a break and to have some fun.

The next day came quickly, and she drove them back to the doctor's office for Brady's third appointment. *She wasn't really expecting anything different today than had happened the other days, but her feelings were unattached and neutral, so it was different for her in a way. She liked this feeling of being on middle ground and being balanced.*

The neurologist called Gina, Brady, and her into his office and asked if either of them had noticed any new developments. They disclosed to him that the edema in Brady's legs and arms had disappeared over night. The doctor rubbed two more dabs of *nitroglycerin* on Brady's arm, then put one more swipe of cream on his opposite arm. Again, they waited for a reaction.

As they were observing him, she noticed that Brady's face appeared to light up and his eyes entertained a look of awareness. Color surfaced on his face and his features moved slightly; an expression was beginning to form. She was riveted by the slow transformation taking place in front of her eyes. Taken in and mesmerized by it, she was

187

unable to shift her eyes away from Brady; she didn't see or hear anything else around her. As something indescribable moved through him, it seemed as though she was feeling what he was feeling.

She saw the beginnings of a seemingly familiar expression slowly move across Brady's face. Spellbound, she watched. As she continued to observe, something tremendous happened–the look on his face transformed into a smile that appeared to grow indefinitely larger. His eyes lit up and his face beamed. Brady's smile, which had been lost in a dormant sleep for seven years, had finally surfaced. His smile had rallied and found its way back into the waking world. Joy shot throughout her being and flooded her in a way she had never felt before. With a cry, tears caught her breath up in a sob. The feeling overcame her so swiftly, she felt as though she had been struck in the heart by a joyous bolt of lightning. She was certain that Brady was experiencing these same feelings as well.

This was the answer to her prayers. Right here, right now; this was the healing miracle manifesting itself in the physical form for her and her daughter to witness while it was occurring in real time. The opportunity to witness a miracle such as this comes around once in a lifetime, if you are lucky. The occurrence of a miracle is something you never forget; it is a flash memory of a rare event in one's life. That moment is filled with a thankfulness and gratefulness from the depths of one's soul.

Brady continued to smile as they stared at him. This was beyond exciting, for this was the first time they had ever seen him smile or show any sign of happiness; up until this very moment, he had been unable to express emotions. She could see the aftermath of his miracle already beginning to strip away and erase the previous seven years of emotional emptiness. This was the miracle for which they had been praying and waiting; it changed their lives. The profoundness of this miracle and how it changed everything for all of them cannot be put into words because it goes beyond the written language—the feeling was impossible to describe.

She and the others left the doctor's office in a much different state than the one in which they had arrived. As the miracle that occurred was still within them, she and her family returned home with overwhelming excitement. The healing that she had hoped for all those years still seemed unbelievable and surreal to her. *Was it real? It didn't seem possible, and yet, it was.* All she had to do was look at Brady to see the proof of the miracle. The changes within him were present and there for her and everyone else to see; she was in awe of his transformation. The fact that she herself witnessed Brady's first smile made it all the more profound of an emotional experience. She was so deeply moved that she knew for the rest of her life she would remain in wonderment and marvel at Brady's miracle; she would never forget how it felt to see him smile for the first time in his life.

At home, the treatment of rubbing nitro-bid on his arms continued. Two weeks later, on Father's Day, something remarkable happened. Brady laughed out loud for the first time ever—and he laughed uproariously, at that. When Brady laughed, his whole body stiffened up with excitement. To see him laugh and show expression was a godsend to her and his parents; he could now have fun and show enjoyment through his smile and laugh. She and the rest of the family enjoyed finding new ways to entertain the silly boy.

She first realized Brady had a dark sense of humor when her son-in-law bumped his sore knee on the edge of a chair and let out a yelp in pain. Brady immediately laughed at his dad. He would also laugh at his brother and sister when they'd get hurt or throw a tantrum. Another way he showed his dark sense of humor was by shedding crocodile tears or pouting if he didn't like something; his dark sense of humor amused her.

She and Gina continued to take Brady for regular visits to the neurologist in Florida, and eventually he added new protocols for him. She noticed that Brady became more comfortable and stronger in subtle ways; people that didn't know him well might not have noticed these changes, but to her and those closest to him, they were easily recognizable and miraculous.

No longer did any of them wonder whether Brady was happy. His smile told them when he was feeling well and that he was enjoying his life, and so were they. Brady's everyday medical issues persisted, but overall, he became stronger and more stable, which made life a little easier to manage.

★★★

Later that same year, Brady needed a surgery on his stomach called fundoplication. Even though he had a feeding tube inserted in his stomach and intestines, severe acid reflux resurfaced, and *coffee grounds* made a reappearance. The acid reflux caused internal bleeding and scarring, which weakened his esophagus and increased the possibility of aspiration.

In order to keep the stomach contents from refluxing back up into the esophagus, the gastrointestinal surgeon wrapped a small segment of Brady's stomach around the lower portion of his esophagus and stitched it in place. While a fundoplication used to require a surgeon to cut open the whole chest cavity, it thankfully now can be performed laparoscopically. A laparoscopic fundoplication was a far less invasive procedure; only three tiny incisions would be made in his abdomen.

She worried about Brady going through this procedure because his respiratory system was still compromised, and a surgery could easily push him over the edge. *Was this it…would this be the time that Brady left us?* She couldn't let herself think this way. *He had come so far–they had come so far–that this couldn't be the time.* Her grandson came through the fundoplication with flying colors, and she felt the release of worry fall from her. He still had to be watched over closely and tended to gently, but she and his mother knew how to do that very well.

★★★

The combination of nitroglycerin treatments and the fundoplication made a visible difference in Brady's health and comfort levels. He became medically stable and comfortable enough to attend school all day, every day. Before the surgery, he only attended school for half a day, and only if he was feeling well. She could see that Brady enjoyed going to school.

The nurse packed his backpack with everything he would need for the day—medicines, formula, syringes, suction pump, oxygen, and saline solution to wet his mouth and nose. Then, just like any other kid, Brady and his nurse would be sent off to school.

For most of Brady's life, his unstable health and severe physical discomfort virtually confined the entire family to their home; but with these latest life-changing treatments, they all experienced a newfound freedom. Even though he still needed to be suctioned and required a constant caregiver, everyone was now able to go places and do things that included Brady. In the summertime, she and her daughter planned outings for the family to enjoy together. She would drive everyone to the zoo, aquarium, amusement park, movies, or the beach. Anything they could think of, they did. She even helped Brady travel to Mexico for vacations.

Mexico: A Reason to Live

After Brady became more stable, she decided it was reasonable enough for her to travel to Mexico and reside there for a while. After all, he had his mother and father living with him if something should happen; knowing this gave her comfort and the confidence to move forward.

She had been staying in Mexico for approximately two weeks and was enjoying her time there just relaxing on the beach. Some of her friends even came for a visit in

LAVINA JEANE PAGE

the warm climate and to soak up the sun. Back home, it was frigid and snowy, so she drank in the moonlit nights and sunny days. Although where she was staying was secluded and remote, she did not mind the seclusion; she liked the alone time in this beautiful place. Life was simple and slow-paced; she had time to reflect on life and let her thoughts come to the surface on their own.

She was lounging on the terrace reading a book; she had wanted to read this one for some time but wasn't previously able to find a long enough opportunity to do so. While reading, she would occasionally look up at the ocean and admire the coconut trees on the beach and the pelicans diving for fish. She thought, *it's amazing how pelicans can see a fish from the height they are flying and then swiftly swoop down and scoop up their catch.*

As she sat there looking out over the water, Brady's essence came to her. Usually he came in a formless vapor; however, this time his being took shape and she could see him clearly. Only this time when he came, it was somehow different from all the others. The moment he appeared she saw and felt, from the core of his being to the core of her being, the agony and depth of his pain, anguish, fear, and confusion. It pierced through her heart and sunk into her bones; her body shook from the intensity with which the sensations struck her. Instantly, the book dropped from her hands onto the terrace floor. She hadn't felt this way since Brady connected with her in the premonition she experienced before his birth. In a sense, this heartbridge was far worse because she could feel Brady's war between life and death; his body was a raging battlefield in unknown territory. He was a spirit prisoner

193

residing inside this body of a child, not understanding what was happening to him.

Something was terribly wrong, and she had to find out what it was. She attempted to calm herself down so she could *feel* into what was happening to him. This was a difficult task because Brady's essence was with her and she was still seeing and feeling the gravity of his situation.

She was finally able to see that he was not in his bed at home where he would normally be. She was quickly guided to a hospital room where she saw him lying in a bed. She became alarmed at the sight of him in a hospital bed with tubes down his throat, since he hadn't been hospitalized in nine years, and immediately called her daughter to find out what was going on. Her daughter disclosed to her, "yes, Brady is in the hospital; he's in grave condition."

She recounted to her daughter what she was experiencing, and that Brady was with her. The entire time that she was speaking with Gina, Brady's cries of pain and confusion were moving throughout her searching for comfort. Her inability to articulate what the spirit and body suffers in a time of such magnified extreme crisis is because that suffering goes beyond the mere words of our experience. Those descriptions available to us are simply words, with no comprehension of what they mean or the feeling behind them. Our bodies and spirits can cry out in pain, be confused, be afraid, feel alone, need love, fight for life, or beg for death. What she *saw* and felt came from a higher realm than hers, and it came with feeling, seeing, and a clear knowing of what her grandson was going through.

The days that Brady was with her, she did the one and only thing she could think of to do…she held him in her heart and in her spirit arms and rocked him; loved him. She told him repeatedly how much she loved him and all the ways in which she cherished and needed him. She told Brady that if he could hang on a little longer, everything would be all right; he would be all right. She reminded him of how much everyone adored him and how he was their guiding star—especially hers. She expressed to him how grateful she was for all the times he had guided her and went on to list them. She told him that he had always been there for her and that she was here for him now, she would stay with him.

The days came and went, each running into the next, as she held him in her arms. It was in her body and spirit that she suffered in Brady's pain, alongside him, during that period. She cried with him those days too, and her heart broke when she knew it was unbearable for him to withstand any more suffering. She knew what she had to do, as hard as it would be. She told Brady that even though she loved him beyond measure, if he wanted to leave, he could. She assured him that it was okay to let go and that she understood, as did his parents. He had been in their lives much longer, years beyond, what he was supposed to be; she declared this to him many times as she cried with him, for him, and for herself. She would feel the loss of his absence in her life, but she understood if he wanted to go. She would be at peace.

The month dragged on until one day she *knew* something had changed. Brady's presence had slowly faded, and she was no longer experiencing the intense feelings of pain, turmoil, fear, and confusion. She grew anxious about not knowing if he had decided to stay or leave; she had to know what was going on. She saw that he wasn't in his hospital bed anymore and grew even more distressed; she was afraid that Brady had decided to depart from this world. While she didn't sense as though he had, she was unaware of what had happened and was becoming more frantic by the minute not knowing.

She finally was able to get a phone call through to her daughter, Gina. She told her that Brady was no longer with her, nor was he in the hospital bed. She asked her daughter where Brady was, and Gina happily reported that they had brought him home from the hospital that morning. When an exquisite wave of relief lifted her spirits, she knew that she had been blessed yet again, and so had he. Brady had decided to stay a while longer; the turbulent war between life and death was over for now. The strength of his warrior spirit had overcome what could easily have gone the other way.

★★★

Brady had changed her and the rest of the family in various ways throughout the years he was with them. He was a spiritual master disguised as a child, guiding her and his family with the light he held within himself; and he did it all without uttering a word. As she was writing her fairytale, she realized Brady had helped her to overcome, and make peace with, her own near-death experience and put it in the past.

Knowing that the nursing situation was taxing for Brady, she flew home as soon as she could. Due to the stress he was under, he was having a difficult time recovering. She felt that the nurses were being overly cautious of his care, which was understandable, but it was causing him anxiety nonetheless. She felt that he needed some time away from everything to improve his chances for a complete recovery, so she suggested to Gina that they take Brady to Mexico for a month to provide him with a change of scenery and energy.

Gina agreed, but was concerned about being able to manage such a trip with him and his siblings. She assured her daughter that together they could do it, and that it was necessary for the vulnerable boy to recuperate. They made all the arrangements necessary and prepared everything that would be essential for a trip such as this.

They made a schedule in which the nurse would care for Brady at night, she would care for him during the day, and Gina would care for him in the evening until the nurse came back on duty. She was nervous, and so was Gina, about carrying out this plan; but they were determined once they had made the decision to do it. Everyone thought she and her daughter were foolish to have considered taking Brady so far; the nursing staff even whispered amongst themselves that taking him to Mexico would never be possible.

★★★

The time for Brady's big trip finally arrived and they were ready to go; it could not have come too soon for anyone. Everything went smoothly as they flew to Mexico without a hitch; nothing was lost or forgotten, and Brady flew as if he knew that he was going somewhere special to heal.

The first day that they arrived at the beach house, she arranged everything for her grandson to rest comfortably on the terrace. She made sure that he would be facing the pool and the ocean, and then assembled blankets and pillows on the lounge chair. Brady would be able to feel the ocean breeze on his face and maybe, just maybe, he would be able to hear the birds and pelicans. She wasn't sure how much he was able to detect sound, but she was hopeful that he would hear the singing birds.

Her daughter brought Brady over to her house and laid him down on the lounge chair. She made sure his suction pump was charged and ready, then she sat it beside him for when she needed to use it. After she applied sunscreen to his skin, he was ready to relax by the pool for the rest of the day.

As she sat beside Brady, she looked at him throughout the day; she noticed that he was glowing and had the most amazed and serene look on his face. To her, it appeared as if he felt like he was in heaven; she knew it was the right decision to bring Brady to Mexico.

Brady never cried or fussed as he did at home; he just laid there basking in the beauty of it all, as though his soul were content being in this place. Every day he rested in the lounge chair on her terrace. She watched him as he lay there in this altered state of beauty, with a glow emanating from his face and body. It filled her heart with love to see him healing and to realize that he had decided to stay and give her and the family more time with him.

She was happy and thankful that they were able to give him the time to heal in this quiet, beautiful place with the sun and ocean breeze. He deserved it, after all the pain and suffering through which he had been. From the time he was born, he never had it easy; his life had been a struggle with severe pain and insurmountable disabilities to live with. She pondered these things as she watched him; *what did Brady and others like him have inside of them that made them different? That made them continue on, in spite of their circumstances? She thought, there must be a deep will to live, to stay with family. A survival instinct must kick in when the body loses its strength to go on. She believed that one's spirit drove them on when it was necessary to do so, and one has no choice but to move with their spirit when it calls.*

As the days came and went, she could see that Brady was growing stronger. When she felt he was healthy enough, she thought it would be a fun idea to put him in her chest-deep swimming pool. Gina very cautiously and slowly lowered Brady down into her arms as she was standing in the pool. She held him close to her and walked him around the pool for a short period but was careful not to overdo his first time. She wanted him to have just a taste of the cold water to see if he would enjoy it. His laughter echoed across the sandy beach as he made it clear that he loved being in the cold pool. She sensed that he liked the way the water buoyed his arms and legs up, enabling him to feel free in the movements of the water. From then on, every day Gina would lower him into the pool with her and she would move him around in playful motions.

Their month in the sun and water had concluded and it was time to return home. Brady had a complete turnaround in his physical and mental health; she felt that without this time in secluded beauty, he would not have recovered as well. She also sensed that this trip had given him the will to prolong his time with his family. Brady felt good and looked well; with a healthy glow about him, he was happy, and so was she.

★★★

Her unspoken connection to Brady continued to grow stronger throughout the years. If she were having difficulty making a decision about something, he would come to her in a presence that was not tangible yet would somehow connect her to the information he wanted to convey.

One time, Brady was with her at an energy healing seminar in California. There were multiple levels of energy healing workshops and she had taken the first two but was undecided about the third. She was sitting outside on a break, pondering whether or not to take the third level, when Brady's spirit appeared in his usual way and directed her to sign up for it. She *knew* it was Brady–she always knew when it was him. She never questioned this because it was just a *knowing* for her.

Sometimes she wished she had kept a journal of all the occasions his spirit had come to her when she needed advice. Although she had written journals through the years, they were not specific to her experiences with Brady, and after a time she would gather them up and rip out all the pages. There was something about another person reading her journals and being privy to her private reflections that she feared. She thought, *maybe what she feared was potential judgment in what they might read; especially if someone else were* mentioned in the journal. *She didn't want to hurt anyone by permanently chronicling her deepest thoughts on paper.* So, she continued to destroy her journals, and always felt better after she did. She supposed, *she felt better because in her mind these written words were in the past. They meant nothing to her now; whatever frame of mind she was in at the time that she wrote them was over and forgotten.*

Healing Brady's Unseen Injuries

For the next few years, Brady had a new lease on life. He still had his bad moments, but they weren't life-threatening; it was during these times that she would practice energy healing on him. Occasionally, she would even lay beside him in his bed, so he would know she was there for him; she hoped that she comforted him in some way.

Her bedroom adjoined Brady's bedroom, which pleased her. She could hear everything that was going on with him at night, and if she heard him having a difficult time she would go into his bedroom and help the night nurse. She stayed with him until whatever was bothering him was sorted out and he was resting comfortably again.

★★★

Gina continued to search for homeopathic treatments, therapies, and medicines that might help Brady be more comfortable; dolphin assisted therapy was one such finding. This was something that seemed like fun to the out-

201

side world, but to her it was more than that. Their first experience with this treatment was an excursion to the Florida bay, during which a dolphin swam up and touched Brady's toes. While on the trip they decided to incorporate a variety of healing options and arranged for him to also receive "four hands" physical therapy with two therapists. After that encounter, he slept all day and night without oxygen–Brady's nurses were amazed.

Physical therapy seemed to make him feel more comfortable, so Gina hired a private physical therapist to come to the house and work with him once a week. After seeing him for several years she began doing something different with Brady's therapy. The therapist had learned a technique called myofascial release therapy that appeared to be helping his scoliosis, even if ever so slightly.

It was now 2012, Brady was fifteen, and her daughter found a myofascial release therapy clinic in Pennsylvania that she hoped would provide him with more comfort. Myofascial release is a therapy which releases trauma that has become trapped in the fascia tissue surrounding our muscles and organs due to physical or emotional injury. Once released, it brings about healing from whatever the issue pertained to; this healing could be on any level–physical, spiritual, or emotional. *Myofascial release seemed like a worthwhile therapy for Brady to have, God knows his traumatic life could certainly use some release,* she thought.

Brady had been doing well and had gained weight–eight pounds to be exact–so she and her daughter decided it was best to drive his adapted van to the therapy clinic she found nearby. She drove everyone to the town where the facility was located, and they checked into their hotel rooms to ready themselves for a two week stay. She liked going on these excursions and so did Brady's brother and sister. She and her daughter always found some unique and enjoyable things for everyone to experience as a way to break up the monotony of doctor or therapy appointments.

The first day at the clinic, Brady was thoroughly examined; measurements were taken of every part of his body. Everything about him was noted, written down, and checked out; there wasn't one part of him that was not assessed. She was impressed by their presence, compassion, and commitment to doing a good job. Now that everything was documented, therapy would begin.

Not only were there three to four therapists and interns working on Brady at one time, but his therapist from home even came to assist. After the third day, some of the therapists needed to continue their work with other patients as well; when they needed an extra hand, they would ask for her or her daughter's help. Once the therapists guided her through the process she found the therapy intriguing and wanted to learn more.

With her hands, she applied pressure on the muscle she was directed to; not hard pressure, but just enough to where she felt a firmness under her palms or fingers. She got the hang of it quickly. When she pressed down on a muscle for a brief period—four to five minutes—she could feel Brady's fascia tissue slowly give way; as it let go, it felt as though her fingers were moving through soft butter. She continued this process through various layers of the muscle until she sensed that all possible fascial restrictions had been released.

She could feel the pain or the issue that the muscle was holding, and when it would release she felt a healing taking place. It was amazing to her the different ways that the body can talk. She knew that the body was alive and could feel things, but she had never experienced anything like this before. She was so in tune with a muscle that it told her the way in which it hurt and how it felt on each level of release that it went through as the healing took place. During this process of healing she would have a wonderful, warm sensation of love and joy move throughout her body; this feeling confirmed to her that the healing was, indeed, taking place.

During the therapy sessions, Brady took on the most blissful, otherworldly look. This was the same tranquil existence she had seen him embody in Mexico while he was recovering; he was in an altered state of absolute euphoria. After his therapy for the day was finished, he stayed in this state of blissfulness and slept well. She could tell that he looked forward to these sessions; their connection was so close that she could pick up on what he felt or wanted without speaking.

She loved seeing Brady experience this peace and comfort. When she looked at her grandson it was as though she saw him in complete wholeness—body and spirit in balance and harmony. It was an eternal spiritual wholeness that radiated out from within him. She would stand there and look at him while he laid on the massage table, enthralled by what this meant to her. *Was this spiritual wholeness something she could achieve in her lifetime like he did?*

Even though on the outside his body was a telling sign that it was not what it should be, he had overcome and gone beyond the physical. She had always known that he was more than his physical presence when he came into their lives. He was there to teach them that we can go beyond–we are capable of going deeper than what we see on the outside. There is a whole other world inside of us that holds the stars and the light of the universe. We have the ability to touch the stars inside of ourselves and feel them explode outwardly as they fall on others in blessings of love.

Brady was here to guide his family in this direction to learn compassion, perseverance, and how to love on a deeper level. He taught her to go beyond the physical and how to go inside of herself to find the treasure chest of gifts that are ours to claim, own, and use. It may have taken her a while to see this, but once she did, it was an epiphany for her. The way he had guided her through the years in his unspoken way was proof that he lived from a higher consciousness than she did.

She and her daughter were so impressed with myofascial release therapy that they decided to attend a week-long workshop in Arizona. Their mindset was that together they could incorporate this type of therapy into the energy work they were practicing on Brady to alleviate his physical discomfort. They felt that he needed this therapy most of all now, because his spine had a curvature of about seventy-five degrees and the scoliosis was putting pressure on his lungs and organs. This curvature only added to Brady's respiratory problems; he began having intermittent episodes of turning blue, which he had never previously experienced.

She and her daughter would find willing friends and

relatives to practice on to improve their healing skills. When she worked on others, she found that there was always a subtle healing that took place for her also. It was the icing on the cake when the healing transferred to her too. She didn't always know specifically what the healing was for her, but it didn't matter; she loved the sensation that spread throughout her being when it happened. It was a feeling of love, of feeling lighter in some way, that she couldn't quite identify.

★★★

One day, while looking through the kitchen window at her daughter's house, she saw Brady and his nurse sitting outside by the pool. He was in his wheelchair and the nurse was standing beside him; they were both facing her direction, so it was easy to see them. Brady didn't have the strap on that held his head in place, so his head kept flopping down onto his right shoulder. It appeared to her as if every time his head fell over, the nurse pushed it back up quickly in annoyance. She knew that this nurse was a nice woman and had been with Brady for a few years, so she doubted that what she was seeing take place was out of irritation.

While she was watching, she questioned herself and wondered, *had she ever acted in annoyance toward Brady when she was taking care of him? She felt that maybe she could have. She hoped that this wasn't true, but still she felt bad in the possibility that she had.* She had a very protective streak and would never allow anyone to mistreat Brady, including herself. She knew that she sometimes failed to see beyond his physical condition, especially when he was having a rough day and there was more involved in his care. She thought to herself, *I'll try to catch myself and be aware of the times when I act out in annoyance toward Brady, or anyone else for that matter.* If she caught herself about to act irritated, she would make herself stop and look at him until she felt a stirring inside of her heart; stop until she could *feel* him, and hopefully he was experiencing the same.

There was a hint of guilt hidden inside her though; *maybe there was a time that she wasn't as aware and unconsciously treated Brady as if she was frustrated.* She prayed that she hadn't ever treated him that way.

Many thoughts crossed her mind as she stood in the kitchen watching. *This glimpse through the window acted as a mirror—it was a reminder of how easy it is to lose sight of the person inside; a reminder to check oneself and to act with compassion.* Still looking out the window, she stood there considering all of this. She silently apologized to Brady for any times she may have unknowingly acted indelicate.

A Time of Leaving

She and Gina continued to practice myofascial release therapy and energy healing on Brady, since his quality of life seemed to be improved by the healing work. Then, something began to change for him; he started to have frightening spells where he couldn't cough up mucus. Even though he was suctioned, he couldn't move these secretions up into his throat far enough to cough them out; Brady couldn't breathe when this happened and was experiencing brief periods of suffocation. Sometimes it took her, Gina, and the nurse performing a combination of rapping him on the back, suctioning him, and talking to him to bring him back to life.

In the beginning, the alarming bouts only occurred sporadically, and it was fairly easy to get Brady through them. Right after she and Gina returned home from the myofascial release therapy workshops, these spells of turning blue grew much closer together. Although they always managed to pull Brady out of it with a lot of effort, it was becoming increasingly more difficult to bring him back. When she heard this happening in the night, she would help the nurse pull him out of the episode. Once these attacks became more habitual, either she or Gina always had to be at the house to potentially assist the nurse; if a spell occurred, it now took a minimum of two people to get him through it.

During these fits, Brady would turn blue and go limp, and at times he would even lose control of his bowels. Each time this happened she watched him die, and each time it was only by the grace of God that they pulled him back from the brink of death. *The darkness stood there waiting for him—or was it the light that was waiting? Maybe the darkness was more like the physical form ready to go and the light was what was waiting ahead.* Time stood still for her in these moments—she was in a void of some kind. Deep down on some level, she knew that eventually they wouldn't be able to bring him back. She couldn't face that fact and would push it down in denial; the nearing end was too painful to face.

She tried to perform energy healing on Brady to see if it would help in some way; she leaned over him and with her hands she felt for his energy field. She had trouble finding it and found that Brady's energy was so close to his body she didn't feel any life to it at all. His energy field was empty, and that's when she felt a helplessness hit her. It was as if someone had slapped her in the face with discouragement in the realization that she was unable to help or do much good for Brady. What came to her next was the idea to play heavenly healing melodies for him, so she played soft and soothing angelic music nonstop and felt that it brought him peaceful tranquility in the face of death. She knew that it somehow helped her too.

The disturbing spells lasted longer and longer, and each time it happened she breathed a sigh of relief once she and Gina brought him back. This time was different though—she felt the air in his room flatten and a stillness took over. She could feel his body form begin to melt away as the spark of life that was Brady began to spread throughout his bedroom and into her room. There was a calmness to the energy that was misleading, as though physical death was not present and impending.

She believed that the body is a vehicle in which our spark lives. It resides there for a time and then moves on—this spark doesn't die along with the body. That didn't make it any easier knowing that she was alive and so was he, in this grand play of a physical world. It takes a superior effort of will and strength to overcome the brutally of death and rise above it. She didn't know if she was capable of rising above death; and if she was, it would only be because of the example set by a fifteen-year-old boy—

her grandson, who dove in deep, and did so with the spark and sparkles of light that he was.

In the early morning she heard frantic movement and her daughter's voice emanating from Brady's room; she immediately got up and went to them. He had slipped into a brief coma the previous day and was now experiencing another spell. She knew when she looked at him that this time there was no pulling Brady back–he had reached his limit. His body was tired and couldn't do any more than it had already done. He was ready to let go, ready to move on. Brady had done his job–the play was over. Untethered and free from the body that he had so courageously served his purpose in, Brady quietly slipped out of his form. She felt the death of his body rather than the death of him, of his spark. His essence was still there in his bedroom and her adjoining room; both her daughter and his father felt Brady's presence too. His spirit stayed to comfort them during his transition. A compassionate love from Brady touched each of them, as he knew the loss they were feeling and wanted to console them as they grieved.

His spirit stayed even after his empty form was moved to prepare it–lovingly and honorably–for the viewings and the funeral; and eventually to rest beside his other grandmother. His spark stayed throughout all this preparation; he was here with her and his family, holding their hands and walking with them.   .

★★★

She stood in Brady's bedroom and looked around the

empty space. He had just been with her that very morning and now he was not—he was gone. An emptiness filled her; she missed him being in his physical form. His body was something she could touch and hug; it didn't help that she knew he was alive in spirit.

She didn't want to dwell on Brady's passing any longer, so she went to her room, exhausted and ready for bed. She laid there not thinking about anything, just quietly resting in the dark. She felt her body shifting and taking on another form; she was curious, so she softly watched and waited to see what this shift meant.

Her body slowly morphed into that of an old woman who was covered up with blankets. Her bed transformed into an old wooden bed with a headboard of poor quality and condition, as if from another time. Sitting on a chair beside her bed was an old man who held her hand in his. She knew that he was taking care of her as an old, sick woman. She could feel the deep love the old man felt for her, which filled her heart. This old couple held a mutual love for each other; a devoted and an unconditional love that was deep and enduring through all of time. She also knew the elderly gentleman was Brady in the form of an old man. He was caring for her, just as she had cared for him in this lifetime.

It was of a time long past, and she knew Brady was showing her why they were so connected, and why they could communicate with each other in this life. The room appeared to have light particles floating everywhere and had a crackling energy to it. There was a warmth to the space and she felt the glow and the soothing effects of it simultaneously. She was enthralled and fascinated by what was taking place; nothing like this had ever happened to her before. While recognizing the truth in her emotions, she laid there and allowed the feelings and sensations to move through her being.

She understood that Brady had set up their connection before he was born not only to show her how his life was going to be, but also to reveal to her that this connection was not bound by the constraints of time. She had put the question of why to rest a long time ago; early on she accepted the fact that there were some things of which we just don't have an understanding. The reasons or purposes are sometimes left a mystery for us to wonder about and then let go of. She was ecstatic to have an answer after twenty years; it all made perfect sense to her now—the way they could communicate with each other by creating a heartbridge.

Just as she had morphed into the old sick woman, she slowly returned to her own form, as did her surroundings. The light particles that had filled her room, however, remained. She laid there taking in the beauty of this—his parting gift to her. She was overwhelmed with joy that something such as this could even happen. She wanted to take it all in and never forget the feelings that came with this wonderful gift because she knew that soon enough the experience would seem as if it never happened. It had though; and while the impression may fade somewhat, this was something she would never forget.

Holding Pattern

The plane had been in a holding pattern for fifteen years. She was looking out the airplane window when she heard the landing gear go down and the pilot's announcement for their final descent. After being on the plane for all these years, she didn't want to get off; neither did Gina or her family. They had made this their home and rearranged everything to their liking to create the most comfort for their family; room had been made in their lives for unexpected circumstances. The entire family had grown flexible to the changes that had to be made in traveling this way–they became accustomed to and embraced them.

In the beginning, when they boarded this unexpected flight, it had taken some time to get used to the unusual journey and understand the workings of it; but they all worked together as a group in order to keep everything running smoothly. They learned so much, especially from the one young passenger who turned out to be their teacher. He taught them what true compassion and unconditional love was.

Over the years, they grew in strength and character during the holding pattern the plane was in. Even though they never knew when the plane was going to land, the young passenger remained courageous and brave in the face of adversity throughout the entire flight.

One at a time, she and the others very slowly stepped off the plane. In departing, each one of them turned and looked back at the aircraft that had been their home for far more years than they had expected it to be. As they looked on, they could see one lone face peering out through an airplane window at them. Looking out the window, the young passenger hung on to each of them as they left. He had a new unexpected adventure to go on and would not be leaving with them. They waved their farewells and kisses to him as they left. Not ready to break the hold of his stare, they stood together on the tarmac in the comfort of each other as his plane took off.

They didn't know what lied ahead for them now–they felt adrift. He had been the center of their lives; while they were together, he had taken on the lead role of being their teacher. It occurred to her that he must have thought they were ready to be on their own now; that she and her family could be self-guiding in the learning of deeper meanings and depth of unconditional love. This thought somewhat comforted her.

She then thought, (*or was it his thought?*) *of how he had swum with the dolphins, his excitement of being carried up the Mayan ruins in Mexico, the first time he smiled, the amusement park rides that he loved. How he loved the movies and going to the zoo and the other amazing places he had been. He had seen and done some extraordinary things despite his pain and disabilities, and she had done them with him.* With these thoughts her heart opened up and filled with love. She could feel him still with her and knew that he would always be with her. He could whisper to her anytime he wanted to and she to him in the way they best knew how. Their life together felt like a fairytale to her when she reflected on it. *All the fantastic things that had happened were like a dream– did they really happen? Yes, she knew they did!*

The Fairytale Ends

Finished with the fairytale, she laid down her old and worn golden pen. She picked it back up and held it *in her hand, as if poised to write more. No, this truly was a fairytale and should end as it did,* she thought. *An unbelievable fairytale, and yet there was truth in it too.*

As she held the golden pen in her hand, she could have sworn it began humming in a soft whisper. When she looked at the special pen, it started to glow and radiate the most magnificent golden hue she had ever seen.

A memory flashed in her mind…it was of her father giving her this artifact when she was sixteen years of age. The vision came with such swiftness that she nearly dropped the golden pen. She saw that as her father handed her the pen it was glowing in the same brilliant manner that it did now. He never told her where or how he had acquired it, but he alluded to the fact that it was very rare and of special qualities; she should keep it safely hidden away. She laid the golden pen down. The vision faded just as quickly as it had appeared, and it no longer glowed. She was intrigued by the mystery of this artifact but felt it best to play detective another day.

She got up from her desk, more than ready for her treadmill workout. *Stretching her legs out would feel good after sitting for so long,* she thought. As she walked toward the treadmill she asked herself, *why did I write this in a fairytale style? It wasn't really; it was a true story. My story. A telling of how my grandson and I could whisper to each other through spirit.* She called their whispers, *"Signals on Fire."*

She now believed that when she saw the book which read *FAIRYTALES*, the vision only meant that writing in fairytale style would allow her to distance herself just enough to write her story. Satisfied that she understood, she put her earbuds in and stepped on the treadmill.

Threads of Gold
The light comes in shining bright,
To wash away all fears,
Great songs are sung as trumpets blow,
Awakening all that are near.
Threads of gold connect our hearts,
To touch and hold love dear.
Great passion comes from threads of gold,
To serve our purpose, once we've been told.
No longer do we tread alone,
When threads of light touch our souls.

The Golden Pen
The golden pen lies in a glow,
Waiting for the script to begin.
Quiet mystery of unknown,
Intrigue the writer's pen.
Words come forth in easy flow,
To lighten the hearts of each its own.

Author's Note

It seems to me that with the cutting-edge medical avenues and alternative methods of healing available to us, combining the two alongside of each other gives us a more balanced approach to heal the body, mind, and spirit.

Thinking outside the box for new and innovative therapies benefits everyone. The ultimate goal is to live and sustain life in the most comfortable and best way possible.

Opening up our minds to the wonder of this approach, and continuing to seek the expansion of enlightenment, can bring about an amazing discovery of self and healing.

95453296R00121

Made in the USA
Lexington, KY
08 August 2018